CW00687150

1993

Long Reining

Philippe Karl

Translated by Anthony Dent

A & C Black · London

The illustrations in this book arise from exercises performed between May 1988 and January 1989, thanks to the devotion and efficiency of the staff of the audio-visual section of the French National School of Equitation.

Photographs by A. Laurioux.

Videotape by G. Petiteau.

The horses were in the care of R. Mercier.

The photographs used in this book feature the following horses:

Chapter IV: Stupéfiant de Retz, Selle Français stallion, 4 y.o. by Nadir T.B. ex Gypsophile, Selle Français, bred by G. Hourcabie.

Chapter V: Raid II, Selle Français stallion, 5 y.o. by Votez Bien A.A. ex Escadrille, Selle Français, bred by Monsieur Bastin-Lavauzelle.

Chapter VI: Odin, pure bred Lusitano stallion, 8 y.o. by Emir ex Guiza, bred by R. Bouzin.

Published 1992 by A & C Black (Publishers) Ltd, 35 Bedford Row, London, WC1R 4JH

First published 1990 in France by Editions Maloine, Paris
© Philippe Karl 1990 and 1992

ISBN 0 7136 3462 6

A CIP catalogue record for this book is available from the British Library

Typeset by ABM Typographics Ltd, Hull

Photo-engraving : La Compagnie de l'Image, Paris

Printed and bound by BPS, Spain

CONTENTS

PREFACE 5

I HISTORY 7

II ELEMENTS OF EQUINE GYMNASTICS 11
Fundamental mechanic data 12
Properties of the gaits in dressage 14
Balance 15
Anatomy and movement 16
An index of gymnastic progress 20

III EQUIPMENT 23

IV INITIATION 25
The voice 25
Impulsion 26
Elementary driving on the curve
and the straight 27
Elementary change of hand 32
Work in a bridle 34
The figure of eight 36
Jumping single obstacles 40
Driving and handiness over two
obstacles 44
Outdoor schooling of the young
horse 46

V CONSOLIDATION 47
The transitions 48

Yielding with the hindquarters on the
circle 49
The shoulder-in reversed 51
The shoulder-in 52
The head to the wall 54
Equipment required 56
The half-pass 57
Circling with haunches-in 60
Jumping style 62
Conduct, transitions and jumping
style 64

VI BRINGING TO PERFECTION 71
Half-passes 72
The reverse change of hand at the
half-pass 73
The pirouette at the walk 75
Taking off at the canter: the collected
canter 78
Introduction to the pirouette at the
canter 79
Teaching collection 82
Teaching the *Piaffer* 83
Passage 88
Teaching the *Pesade* 90
Work in hand and on the long reins 92

TRADITION AND PROGRESS 94

INDEX 96

To General Pierre Durand
to whom I owe the priceless
good fortune of being admitted
to the École Nationale
d'Équitation.

To Colonel François de Beauregard
to whom I owe the signal honour
of being picked for the
Cadre Noir.

To Monique Bastide
To André Rioton
To Martine, Eglantine
and Valentine

Translator's note
It is accepted that the French language has no precise word for *canter*
(the dictionary's definition is *le petit galop*). The exercises described in
this book are to be performed at a canter, yet the author does not write
au petit galop but simply *au galop* when providing directions on how to
perform them. For the purposes of this book, the French *galop* has been
translated consistently as *canter*.

PREFACE

It is an honour to be asked to write an appreciation of Philippe Karl's book, having had the great pleasure of watching his work on long reins with one of his Portuguese Lusitano horses at Saumur. As his quiet, pleasing work unfolded, I began to realise that here indeed were the makings of a Master in the old sense of the word, poised to bring more understanding to students of equitation in this modern world.

Unfortunately, there are still far too many practical horsemen and women who regard the art of long reining as irrelevant to today's highly competitive equestrian climate. Certainly this art has enjoyed an illustrious epoch at the Cavalry School of Saumur, together with the *haute école* with which, for many, the name of the Cadre Noir has become synonymous. It must not be forgotten, however, that Saumur has always maintained its tradition of sporting riding; such has been the success of French officers in show jumping and cross-country riding, that France has earned more than her share of international medals over recent decades.

This tradition of all-round riding is well reflected in Philippe Karl's book. With exemplary photographs which bring the whole text to life, the section on jumping and forward work adds a broader dimension to the schooling of the young horse. As we progress from basic dressage to lateral work, and finally to advanced work and the fine airs, we are reminded constantly of the importance of balance and lightness. The section on the gaits and the study of motion is written with great clarity and understanding and should motivate many to greater achievement.

In addition to these straightforward explanations, the author generously shares so many of the little secrets associated with the French Classical School which has long enjoyed superiority in the academic field. One can appreciate why Philippe Karl won his prized golden spurs at Saumur and was invited by his chief instructor to join the teaching staff at the École Nationale d'Équitation. A more enthusiastic and experienced instructor would be hard to find.

This book should encourage many more riders to consider long reining for themselves. It is clearly very possible to become acquainted with schooling from the ground; the advantages to the horse of early and subsequent training with no weight on the back must be obvious to all. Inspiringly illustrated, this is a book to be treasured, but above all to be used as a very practical training manual. It should not gather dust on the shelf!

Long Reining offers an open invitation to devotees of the art of classical equitation to explore an alternative method which will actually enhance mounted work. Anthony Dent has rendered all serious riders a great service in translating this book which will surely be added to the long list of French classic works.

Sylvia Loch
President of the Lusitano Breed Society of Great Britain

*'It was not until
the renaissance of literature,
of science and of the arts,
that riding began to be taught
systematically in Italy . . .
So long as there were no
riding schools nor rational
instruction, and as long as
the gentry prided themselves
on their inability to read
or write, the art of riding
made no progress.'*

F. Musany
Propos d'un écuyer *(1895)*

I

HISTORY

The Italian Renaissance was a decisive moment in the evolution of the art of riding. It was from the famous Neopolitan school of Gianbattista Pignatelli that the founder of French academic equitation, Antoine de Pluvinel (1555-1620), re-introduced the use of the pillars in schooling horses.

In his book *L'instruction du Roy en l'exercise de monter à cheval*, Pluvinel shows the young king Louis XIII the importance of the single pillar in making the young horse submissive and supple, and then the excellence of the double pillars in collecting and preparing it for airs above the ground. As an essential technique for schooling from the ground, the pillars were permanently employed throughout the seventeenth century despite certain reservations, expressed notably by the Duke of Newcastle. The Masters of the eighteenth century were to continue on this track; F. Robichon de La Guérnière affirmed in his *L'Ecole de Cavalerie*: 'I regard the pillars as a means whereby not only to bring out the resources, the vigour, the gentleness, the lightness and the balance of a horse, but also as a means of giving these last qualities to those that are not already endowed with them.' But the end of that century saw the gradual abandonment of the single pillar in favour of the lunge, together with a progressive reduction in the use of double pillars. However painstaking the preparation of the horse was, the pillars had the major drawback of militating against forward movement.

Federigo Mazzuchelli (1760-1830), a renowned Milanese teacher, was among those who sought to soften the severity of the limits imposed by the use of the pillars. In his *Elementi di Cavalerizza* – published in 1805

Le Manège Royal
*by A. de Pluvinel.
Work on the
single pillars.*

and a landmark in equestrian literature since it was the first work to prescribe the use of 'driving reins' in the training of the riding horse – he commends it as an accessory to work between the pillars. A young Frenchman, at that time working in the stables of Prince Borghese and who in the years to come was to make quite a name for himself, was an attentive observer of maestro Mazzuchelli . . . his name was François Baucher.

Today, long reins are usually looked upon either as a technique for preparing horses intended for harness work, or else as a subtle means of presentation for the dressage horse already broken to saddle. However, one is justified in thinking

Teaching the Pesade *between the pillars.*

that with the aid of careful progress and some material adjustments, long reins can contribute effectively to the education of the saddle horse.

All techniques of work from the ground bear witness to the same motivations and tend towards similar aims.

1 To establish confidence in situations where the rider is trying to get the horse to accept him simply as a fellow-being. Gradually, the rider obtains the horse's respect, rising in the process to the rank of 'dominant fellow-being'. On foot, the trainer can appear as a 'collaborator' to an incredible degree. So long as he is on the horse's back he is in the position of a 'predator' (i.e. in the typical attitude of a lion or other large feline which attacks horses by jumping on

to the withers and biting the spine, at the same time strangling with the forepaws).

2 To observe and analyse the behaviour of the horse.

3 To teach him the language of the aids before using them from the saddle.

4 To obtain relaxation, suppleness and balance through the practice of gymnastics, without the distraction caused by the weight of the rider.

Compared with other techniques of work from the ground, the long reins are characterised by the following.

1 Greater demands on the part of the trainer (in terms of experience and ability) than with work on the lunge. On the other hand, the opportunities are infinitely richer for the

horse and less constricting than the use of riding reins in whatever fashion. The trainer can give and take, resist and yield, bend to this side or that, just as he can vary at will attitudes, figures and gaits.

2 If they do set up a clearly less subtle relationship between man's hand and horse's mouth than that obtained from the ground by riding reins handled by a trainer walking shoulder-to-shoulder, long reins bring the great advantage of closely controlling the haunches without restricting the impression that the horse depends entirely on the trainer, who remains close to him.

But long reins cannot be a universal cure, any more than other

Training on long reins by Federigo Mazzuchelli's method.

methods of training from the ground. If one can dispense with them easily, it is nevertheless a pity to disregard the practice entirely or underestimate its merits.

The following work proposes to study the various uses of long reins throughout the schooling of the saddle horse, without neglecting any single aspect of it.

INITIATION

Proceeding from the simple to the multiple, long reins may take over the functions of work on the lunge and enrich it in the context of careful schooling. In this way the horse will be submitted to a schooling in the aids as advanced as possible before being ridden, without sacrificing any element of forward motion nor dispensing with jumping obstacles.

CONSOLIDATION

As for the refinement of dressage by transitions and lateral movements, long reins correspond to a stage of training under the saddle. In any case it is always interesting to vary the situations and to watch one's horse being handled with no weight on the back.

PERFECTIONMENT

To the extent that the trainer will have obtained control of his horse's hindquarters and his bringing to hand by assiduous practice of the whole range of exercises on two tracks, and transitions, he can, if required, have recourse to long reins to bring his pupil forward in the art of 'collection'.

II

ELEMENTS
OF EQUINE
GYMNASTICS

Seeing that a major advantage of training horses from the ground lies in the opportunity which it affords to observe the behaviour of the horse, it is imperative that in order to analyse this the trainer should be able to measure by some objective standard.

In one of those lapidary passages of which he was such a master, Maestro Oliveira said: 'There are two things in riding: technique and the soul'. It is obvious that, as with every medium of expression, riding only achieves the dimensions of an art when it can escape from the shackles of technique . . . and to do this one must have attained a high technical level. The sense of animal psychology, tact and sensibility of the trainer can only come into play when grounded on a solid basis of data about the anatomy, the equilibrium and the mechanics of the horse. That fervent admirer of the French School, Gustav Steinbrecht, a distinguished German riding master of the nineteenth century, chose for the title of his work *Equine Gymnastics*.

For a comprehensive study of anatomy and locomotion, I can do no better than recommend Commandant Licart's book *Equitation Raisonnée*. Here I propose more modestly to underline fundamental data on which the most practicable progress in gymnastics can be grounded.

FUNDAMENTAL MECHANIC DATA

According to Commandant Licart's book, it would seem that the first cinematographic study of the gaits of the horse was made by Commandant Chamorin. (The first English one was by Edward Muybridge.) It revealed that motion is closely dependent on undulations of the spinal column: 'This crawling motion, the most elementary method of progression, is still present in the higher vertebrates, even if provided with limbs and whether they go on four legs or on two.' (Licart) These spinal waves are produced both in the vertical and the horizontal plane.

At all three paces the following will be seen.

1 When the legs on one side are parallel, all the vertebrae are drawn together.

2 When the legs on one side approach each other, the dorso-lumbar vertebrae are hollowed.

3 When the legs on one side are drawn apart, the dorso-lumbar vertebrae are rounded.

4 At the walk and the trot, the symmetrical gaits, the waves in the spinal column, produce a series of S's and

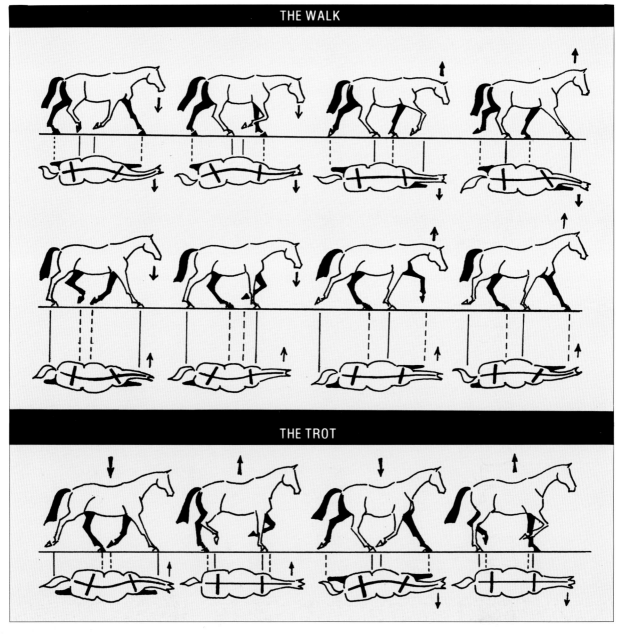

THE WALK

THE TROT

Diagram from Équitation Raisonnée *by Commandant Licart. (Undulations deliberately exaggerated.)*

inverted S's. The hind legs are brought one-by-one under the mass of the body. The dorso-lumbar vertebrae are concave on the side where the hind leg is under the horse, and thus convex on the side where the hind leg is extended. At the walk and the trot, it is the undulations in a horizontal plane which prevail.

5 At the canter, the vertebral undulations in a horizontal plane are asymmetrical and much reduced. They form a series of S's on the left foot, and of reversed S's on the right foot. With the hind legs coming under the body almost simultaneously at the canter, it is the undulations in a vertical plane which prevail.

6 The length of the stride depends on the fullness of the undulations of the spine, horizontally at the walk and the trot, vertically at the canter. Therefore, for the trainer, priority must be given to preserving and developing this flexibility of the spine in all directions.

7 Since, after all, absolute symmetry does not exist in the animal world, all horses show a natural inflexion which is more or less marked, whichever side it is. This is not without influence on the whole of their movements. In the case of a natural inflexion to the right, the horse tends to traverse to the right, pushes with the left hind rather than bringing it under him, brings the right hind under him rather than pushing with

it, and takes right-handed corners wider and left-handed corners more narrowly.

Since the full benefit of the locomotive apparatus is only obtained when going straight, only horses whose spinal waves are produced symmetrically will go quite straight. Thus training consists primarily in straightening up. 'The horseman with all the perfection of his art spends his life correcting this imperfection'. (D'Auvergne)

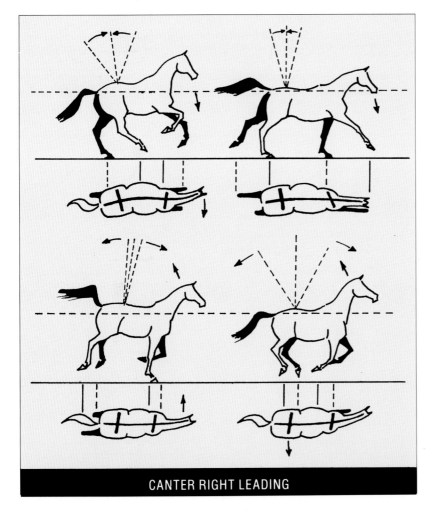

CANTER RIGHT LEADING

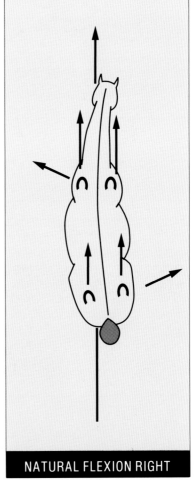

NATURAL FLEXION RIGHT

PROPERTIES
OF THE GAITS
IN DRESSAGE

THE WALK

At this gait (which is symmetrical and has four equal phases) there is no suspension, no moment at which all four feet are off the ground. This is the succession of footfalls: near fore, off hind, off fore, near hind, etc.

STRIDE

Phase	Base
1	Three-footed, off fore
2	Diagonal right
3	Three-footed, near hind
4	Lateral, near
5	Three-footed, near fore
6	Diagonal, left
7	Three-footed, off hind
8	Lateral, off

Therefore, at the walk the horse has great stability, since the stride consists of four three-footed bases separated by four two-footed bases (two diagonal and two lateral). The head and neck play an active part, as balancers (hence 'nodding').

Slow, calm and steady, this gait allows the rider to give his signals with great precision to a receptive horse. At the walk, too, it is easiest to overcome resistance and to relax. However, the rider can only have slight control of balance when the weight of the horse – which is still firmly supported on two or three legs – cannot be shifted easily at this gait. Besides, the natural play of the head and neck, inseparable from a lively gait, makes for a lack of fixity in the forehand which hampers the *bringing to hand*. To base dressage on this gait would incur the risk of sacrificing impulsion to precision.

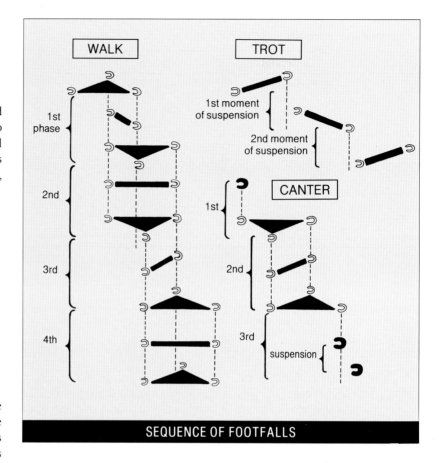

SEQUENCE OF FOOTFALLS

THE TROT

This is a springing gait, symmetrical and diagonal, with two moments of suspension. Thus, bouncing from one diagonal to the other, the balance is rather unstable, but constant and dynamic, so that the rider can act on it effectively. Furthermore, the trot is the only gait in which the forehand is naturally fixed. This characteristic is suited to the basic gait for the study of bringing to hand that favours forward motion and, indeed, proceeds from it.

Three simple remarks confirm the essential role played by the trot in re-establishing the balance of the horse.

1 The study of motion shows that all changes of gait take place on a diagonal basis

2 In backing, the horse naturally takes diagonal steps as he walks backwards, thus pushing his weight on to the hindquarters.

3 If, under the influence of some stimulus, a horse moves without leaving the spot, he spontaneously takes up the lateral posture by pawing the ground.

Thus nature clearly shows that the horse controls his balance most effectively from a diagonal posture; that is why the trot is incontestably a key gait in equine gymnastics.

THE CANTER

This is a leaping, swinging gait in three phases, with one moment of suspension. The canter is marked by the fact that the legs on one side are (for two-thirds of the time) in advance of those on the opposite side. Thus, we distinguish between the

Succession of footfalls		
	Canter right	Canter left
1st phase	Left hind (1)	Right hind (1)
2nd phase	Diagonal left (2)	Diagonal right (2)
3rd phase (suspension)	Right fore (3)	Left fore (3)
	Left hind, etc.	Right hind, etc.

Succession of footfalls		
	Canter right	Canter left
Weight borne	Left hind	Right hind
Weight borne	3-footed left fore	3-footed right fore
Weight borne	Diagonal left	Diagonal right
Weight borne	3-footed right hand	3-footed left hind
Weight borne	Right fore	Left fore
	Suspension phase, etc.	Suspension phase, etc.

canter with right foot leading, and that with left foot leading.

At the canter, the head and neck play a vital part as a counterweight. The neck is extended and the head lowered when the horse swings his weight from the quarters to the shoulders and they both come up again when the weight moves back on to the quarters.

If the canter is not *a priori* a gait favourable to the practice of bringing to hand, it does present the advantage of exercising the whole upper part of the horse by alternate bending and stretching. However, as a working gait the canter poses various problems.

1 Foothold and balance fluctuate and are therefore hard to master.
2 Speed tends to excitement, which quickly leads to fatigue.
3 Uneven working of the limbs accentuates lack of lateral flexibility and prevents straightness of movement.

For all these reasons it seems

one must consider the canter much more as a means of testing progress achieved at the walk and the trot, than as a basic dressage gait.

To sum up briefly the general use of the gaits in the education of the riding horse, one may lay down that it is expedient:

1 to begin with the walk
2 to study and improve with the trot
3 to verify and confirm with the canter.

JUMPING

Jumping obstacles benefits all horses, whatever the purpose of their training. This exercise develops the horse's morale, his spirit of attack; but it also affords an irreplaceable gymnastic exercise which:

1 contributes to dexterity and balance
2 strengthens the quarters
3 loosens and bends the whole upper frame from ears to tail.

BALANCE

'The juggler balancing a peacock's feather on the tip of his nose constantly shifts the point of support to keep the feather upright and thus prevent it falling. And the feather bending this way and that forces the man carrying it to walk.' (Ch. Raabe, 'Study of balance in superimposed bodies')

'. . . the easier the shifting of weight in all directions, the more perfect the equilibrium. By virtue of this principle we say that the horse is 'balanced' when the slightest of signals from the rider will suffice to alter at will the distribution of its weight on the columns that sustain it.' (Faverot de Kerbrech)

One could quote countless others confirming that 'submission, lightness and balance' are inseparable equestrian concepts.

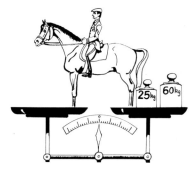

Experiments carried out by Baucher and General Maurice, later confirmed by Captain de Saint-Phalle, give valuable indications of the static equilibrium of the horse under the saddle.

Two scales specially arranged enable one to record the weight borne by the forehand (Fh) and the hindquarters (Hq) respectively.

In all horses a surcharge on the forehand is clearly evident. It can be expressed thus:

$$\text{Coefficient of surcharge:} \frac{Fh-Hq}{\text{total weight}}$$

Measurements recorded for several subjects give the following average limits.

$$\frac{1}{10} < \text{surcharge} < \frac{1}{8} \text{ total weight}$$

The presence of a rider increases this imbalance:

$\frac{2}{3}$ of his weight on the forehand
$\frac{1}{3}$ of his weight on the quarters

Depending on whether the rider causes the head to be lowered to the full or raised to the full, the result is a displacement of $\frac{1}{25}$ of the total mass forwards or backwards.

This data explains the clumsiness of the young horse under the saddle and confirms that a firm seat and an acute sense of balance are essential to the horseman. Finally, they reveal that the head and neck act as a counterweight and that consequently all changes of gait and balance must be linked to variations in the attitude of the forehand.

For example, with a horse weighing 540 kg and a rider weighing 75 kg:

natural overweight on the forelegs:
$$\frac{540}{9} = 60 \text{ kg}$$

overweight due to presence of rider:
$$\frac{75 \times 1}{3} = 25 \text{ kg}$$

total overweight: 85 kg
variations due to the position of the head and neck ± 22 kg

In movement, if this balance is favourable to speed, it works against accurate control of the horse's strength by the rider. The raising of the head is an important factor in adjusting balance . . . necessary but not sufficient on its own.

The complete submission of the horse, its handiness, is expressed by mobility in every direction, and so the trainer will seek to set up an harmonious distribution of weight between the shoulders and the haunches. Only in a state of unstable balance (centre of gravity placed on top of a supporting shortened polygon) can a heavy mass be subject to the movement of another, lighter mass, the latter resting on the former.

This unstable balance can only be induced by the raising of the forehand simultaneously with the bringing of the hind legs under the body: this is the classic definition of 'collection'.

ANATOMY AND MOVEMENT

The elements determining movement are as follows.

1 The dorsal ligament connecting the head to the sacrum and which is fixed to the spinal processes of all the vertebrae. It braces the dorso-lumbar region and extends along the neck where it becomes elastic and keeps the forehand erect.
2 The inferior ligament is also joined to the vertebrae, from the sacrum to the lower third of the dorsal

LONG BASE
Balance favourable to speed

SHORT BASE
Loss of speed
Gain in handiness

UNSTABLE BALANCE
Mobility in all directions
subject to balance and motivity

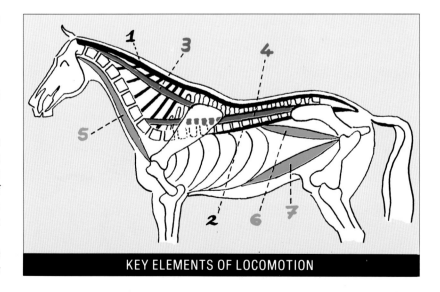

KEY ELEMENTS OF LOCOMOTION

region. It reinforces the dorso-lumbar segment.

3 The splenius muscle turns the forehand and extends the poll.

4 The ilio-spinal ligaments extend the dorso-lumbar-sacral segment and raise the base of the neck.

5 The mastoido-humeral ligaments lower the forehand and bend the neck.

6 & 7 PSOAS and abdominal ligaments serve to flex the lumbar-sacral segment.

THE RAISING OF THE NECK

Consisting as it does of a considerable shifting backwards of weight towards the quarters, the raising of the neck is a tempting means for the horseman to begin re-balancing the horse. In fact, it is relatively easy to bring the horse's head up by vigorous use of the hands. Baucher made this procedure, practised first from the ground and then from the saddle, the starting point of this 'second manner'.

These attitudes imply as follows.

1 At the behest of the hand, the horse contracts the ligaments of the forehand which in turn bring up the head and extend the poll, so that the face approaches the horizontal.

2 The spinal ligament relaxes and no longer braces the base of the neck, which goes slack, the withers sinking between the shoulders.

3 The ilio-spinal ligaments contract to take over the maintenance of the neck in a high position from the dorsal ligament. These factors now combine for the whole top-line to be hollow from ears to tail.

4 The extension of the lumbar-sacral segment brings the pelvis nearer the horizontal, allowing the hind legs to relax but preventing their being brought under the body (as in a bolting horse).

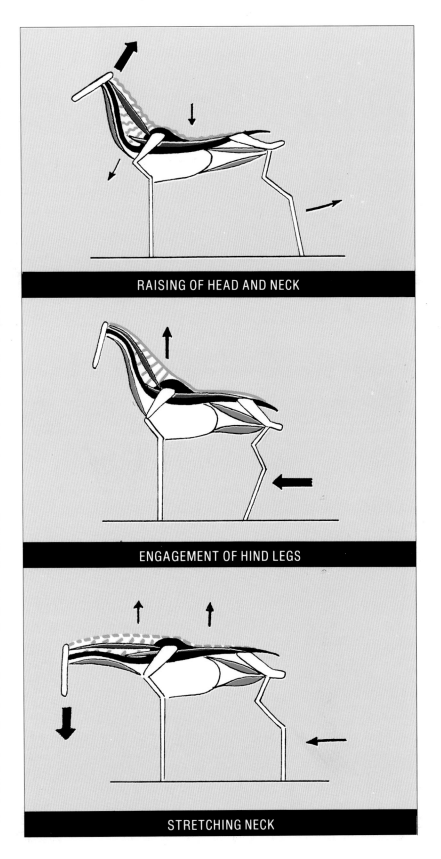

RAISING OF HEAD AND NECK

ENGAGEMENT OF HIND LEGS

STRETCHING NECK

5 The abdominal muscles stretch and the horse tends to stand stretched.

Result

The anticipated adjustment of balance is largely discounted by the hindquarters being extended.

All movement is affected by the state of persistent contraction in the dorso-lumbar region which restricts the scope of play in the spinal column and causes a tendency to a lateral gait (the amble), to a cramped or daisy-cutting trot, and to a slovenly canter. The horse will be walking with his legs and not with his back. He will look stiff and uncomfortable, it will be hard to bring him to hand and keep him so, and his style in jumping will deteriorate.

Natural motion being thus prevented, there is a risk of damaging the physical well-being of the horse and of shortening his life.

Conclusion

There can be no such thing as an harmonious and balanced horse unless the base of the neck is supple.

ENGAGING THE HIND LEGS

By means of the pillars, the Masters of old achieved a highly engaged position of the quarters and so brought their horses to a very firm balance necessary for the practice of airs above the ground (then called 'bounds') which was highly esteemed in those days.

Let us see what results from engagement of the hind legs.

1 The shortening of the abdominal muscles and the PSOAS have their part in bringing the hocks under the body; they cause the lumbar-sacral segment to be flexed and the back to be arched.
2 The stretching of the ilio-spinal ligaments and the heightened ten-

sion of the spinal ligament cause a supple support for the base of the neck.

Result

The persistent state of flexion in the body, back and loins limits the vertebral play in the horizontal plane but enhances it in the vertical one; the horse steps higher and with more spring, even if he gains less ground. The horse becomes more expressive, the walk becomes diagonal, there is a swinging trot (culminating in its stylisation – the *Passage*) and the canter becomes round.

The forehand rises higher, the shoulders are lightened, the horse gains in handiness.

Conclusion

The extension of the muscles of the top-line is an indispensable condition for putting the horse in balance.

Summary

In the context of today's modern saddle horse (without sacrificing either the study of collection, or sporting aims such as jumping), the rider must not exclusively practice: the systematic raising of the head and neck, which results in a hollow back; or the bringing of the hocks under the body, for this is incompatible with the natural development of the gaits and the initial aid to impulsion.

EXTENSION OF THE NECK

If the horse arches the neck forwards and downwards so as to produce any significant prolongation of the back, the face approaching the vertical (as recommended by Commandant Dutilh, écuyer en chef of the Cadre Noir from 1874 to 1877, as the beginning of forward motion), then the mastoido-humerals pull the head downwards by flexing the poll

slightly. The splenius muscles extend and do not resist the elementary bringing to hand. In this attitude, with the face close to the vertical, there is only a slight closing of the poll, which the horse gives willingly. The poll will close progressively, as the neck comes up in the course of collection. This developing flexibility of the poll will allow the rider to excuse the horse from any acceptance of the bridle; most often a simple contact will suffice. Horses with tender mouths will have no cause to recoil; those with hard mouths will be deprived of what makes them heavy on the hand and bores them.

The horse's centre of gravity comes forwards and downwards. This is a balance favourable to the development of the gaits, an attitude which serves to strengthen the natural impulsion of the horse and make him light on his legs, with a great economy of means. We have irrefutable proof of this in *Questions Équestres*, where General L'Hotte reminds us of the infallible efficacy of tight reins applied to inveterate stubborn horses. In fact no horse, even the most dangerously stubborn, will refuse to move forwards when tight reins are pushing the head forwards and loosening the neck. If the balance is favourable, the exercise is obtained with the minimum of restraint and taken without fuss. Thus recourse to whip or spurs is reduced to a minimum, either to overcome idleness or ill will. In this way, one avoids that abuse of all kinds of 'accelerators' which bore or antagonise the horse.

The spinal ligament is stretched to the utmost and pulls on the processes of the vertebrae, running up the base of the neck and stretching the dorso-lumbar region. Because their forward attachments come forwards, the ilio-spinals lengthen. Extension of the neck thus has the merit of solving an essential problem in the gymnastics of the young horse: it prepares him for breaking by encouraging a frame that will enable him to carry a rider without contracting his back. The horse stretches and raises his back just as a climber bows his head and bends his back to take the weight of a heavy, bulky rucksack with a minimum of discomfort and fatigue.

The arching of the dorso-lumbar complex eases the work of the abdominal muscles and thus the engagement of the hind legs. When in motion, this largely compensates for the imbalance caused by the lowering of the head. Stretching the neck prevents the horse from hollowing his back, even in the sustained development of the gaits, and this fits logically into a plan for the mastery of impulsion leading to the study of collection. Apart from this it is a splendid means of conditioning for jumping because it bends the back from ears to tail and thus contributes style by preparing the back to arch on the straight and extend on the curves.

Just as a wooden rod is easier to bend the greater its length, the lengthening of the spine increases the lateral flexibility of the whole horse. If the horse is supple from ears to dock, the vertical waves in the horizontal plane increase in amplitude. The engagement of the hind legs, one after another, being thus facilitated, movements become more sweeping.

Bending of the whole horse encounters less resistance, giving a handier horse even at fast paces.

Conclusion

Practice with the neck extended is indispensable for all horses for various reasons. It is even valuable as kinetic therapy since it arches ewe-necks or other malformations and improves those that are set on too high or too low by pulling them out. It facilitates the progressive study of bringing in hand where the head is set on coarsely. It stretches and sets up backs which are long, weak or loose, and lengthens and supples short backs as well as stiff ones. It takes the weight off weak hocks and strengthens the hindquarter before putting weight on it.

'Whether it be a question of making or re-making a horse, it is always best to begin with stretching exercises'. (Cdt. Licart)

MEANS TO ADOPT IN OBTAINING EXTENSION OF THE NECK

A horse keeps his head up by simultaneous contraction of muscles of the neck. To lower the head, these muscles must be extended again. This is managed by reining to one side. In fact: 'Bending the neck to one side which is incompatible with the simultaneous contraction of the muscles on either side, compels one of them to relax, so that, thus dissociated, their resistance collapses. For anatomical reasons it is impossible for a horse to bend the neck sideways and at the same time hold it up'. (Cdt. Licart)

So it is alternate bending, right and left, which brings the horse to hand and supples it.

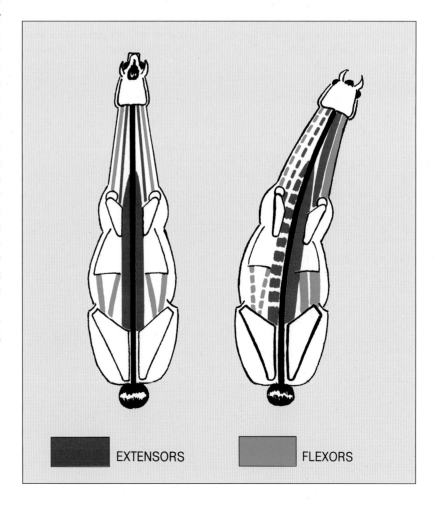

EXTENSORS   FLEXORS

These neck-binding exercises are a foretaste of the bending of the whole spinal column which makes up the basis of a rational equine gymnastic for riding purposes, for the following reasons.

1 The bending of the whole body puts all the muscles of the outer (convex) side at the stretch, thus combating the contractions and resistances whether at the level of the neck, of the back, or of the loins (hollow back).

'When a joint is made to bend, it is not the muscles that operate the flexion that are made more supple, but those that oppose it, because they are the ones that have to yield and relax.' (General L'Hotte)

AN INDEX OF GYMNASTIC PROGRESS

INITIATION

This may be considered as embracing the entire preparation for breaking as well as elementary training under the saddle.

Having first obtained obedience to the voice by work on the lunge, the horse may be gradually intro-duced to the long reins which give him elementary instruction in the aids. Alternately going straight and on the curve, bending to the right and to left, the trainer brings his horse to hand by stretching of the neck. The top-line tensed or arched in forward movement, the horse is now ready to begin the mounting lesson, to learn to carry a man in a relaxed state and to respect the aids.

If the horse adopts a frame under the saddle that conforms to its natural balance, encourages forward movement, stretches the back, improves lateral flexibility and facilitates the start of bringing to hand, he

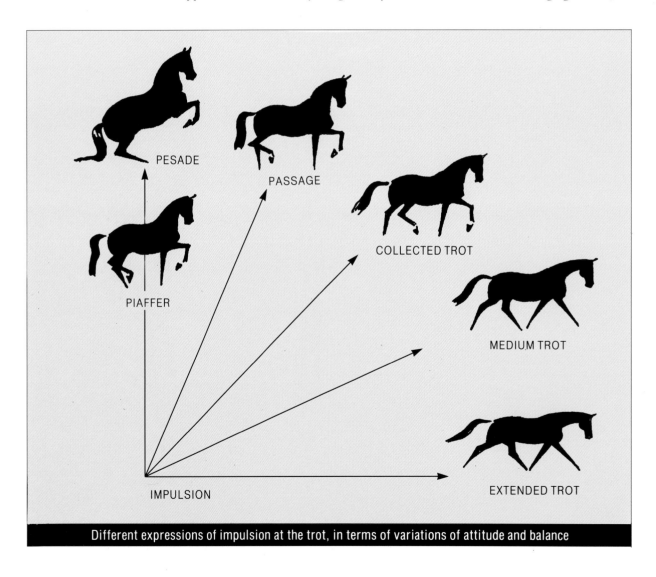

PESADE

PASSAGE

COLLECTED TROT

PIAFFER

MEDIUM TROT

IMPULSION

EXTENDED TROT

Different expressions of impulsion at the trot, in terms of variations of attitude and balance

goes to work without restraint, is not worried about carrying a rider and lets himself be guided. In that case the rider is best able to develop the natural gaits to their optimum of extension and to release maximum impulsion. He profits by increased lateral flexibility and the ability to re-absorb any imbalance in his horse and ensure that the horse begins by going straight. Only progressive transitions in the gaits and from one to another need be practised.

The rider often rises to the trot in order to ease the horse's back. He will only sit down to the trot by easy stages and to the extent that the ex-tension of the neck is not affected by it – proof that the back remains toned up, supple and relaxed under the rider's weight.

At the end of this stage of train-ing the horse ought to be pleasant to ride on the flat and over small jumps, outdoors and in the covered school, at lively paces and over varied country.

CONFIRMATION/ CONSOLIDATION

This means the combination of exer-cises that prepare the horse for train-ing in *collection*.

Previously, due to the extension of the neck, the rider has been able to adjust the top-line of the horse and develop the thrust of its hindquarters at fast paces. Now a judicious progress on two tracks will supple and strengthen the thighs in turn, bring-ing the hind legs alternately under the body. This lesson, improving the capacity of the whole body to bend and equalising the action of the thighs, contributes powerfully to going straight.

Since the hind legs come under the body little by little without diminishing their activity, the back gains in tension and elasticity; con-sequently the progressive raising of

the base of the neck, combined with the bending of the poll, constitutes the flexed position in hand.

If the horse reverses his neck and opens the poll in an attempt to get 'underneath the hand', this shows that he is raising the forehand by contraction of the upper muscles (splenius and ilio-spinal) and not by bringing the hindquarters under him. If the rider is satisfied by this de-ceitful appearance, he will also have to be content with riding a stiff horse with a back that is hollow instead of in the true flexed position. Every time one begins to bring the horse in hand, this can be tested by the capac-

ity to resume the extension of the neck by reverting to a free pace with-out the slightest restraint.

As his balance improves the horse gains more and more mobility and response to the aids. He be-comes lighter; the gaits become more rhythmical; they gain in height and amplitude what they lose in length; they become expressive and sparkling. This style is brought to the gaits in hand, whether at the walk, the trot or the canter.

PERFECTIONMENT

This amounts to an advanced study of collection and leads to the perfor-

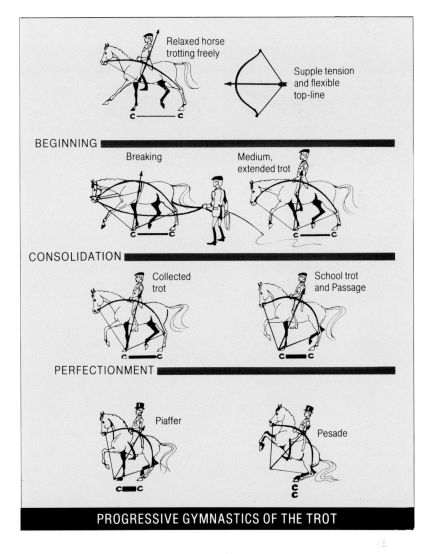

BEGINNING

Relaxed horse trotting freely

Supple tension and flexible top-line

Breaking

Medium, extended trot

CONSOLIDATION

Collected trot

School trot and Passage

PERFECTIONMENT

Piaffer

Pesade

PROGRESSIVE GYMNASTICS OF THE TROT

mance of the airs for which the horse must be well based on his haunches.

The tight turns of the shoulders about the thighs, as well as the transitions repeated at close intervals from forward to reverse movement, serve to settle the horse.

Getting the hind legs under the body, the lowering of the thighs, the arching of the loins and the lightening of the forehand all increase. The power of the hindquarters is expended in upward propulsive force, or in bearing strain. The school trot gives rise to the *Passage*. The *Piaffer* derives from the collected walk. A shortening of the collected canter can develop into the *Terre-à-terre*.

Thus balanced, the tightest turns on the haunches are easily executed, especially the *Pirouette* at the canter.

At the furthest point, the shortening of strides and the lightening of the forehand are such that from the *Piaffer* the horse is able to raise his shoulders and stand for a few moments supported on his bent hocks alone; this is the *Pesade*. 'The *Pesade* is an air in which the horse rears up on the spot without moving forwards, keeping his hind feet still and firm on the ground . . . This lesson is used to prepare the horse to jump with greater freedom, with complete control of his forehand' (F. de la Guérinière)

The *Pesade* may be considered as the culminating point of collection.

III

EQUIPMENT

THE SURCINGLE

Double-buckled, it can be adapted to almost all requirements. Five or six rings on each side increase the options for altering the reins from the lowest to the highest position.

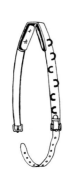

THE LUNGEING WHIP

A short handle about 1.3 m (4 ft) long. A leather lash at least 4 m (4.4 yds) long. The whole, not at all bulky, enables one to reach the horse 6 m (6.6 yds) away if necessary.

DRESSAGE WHIP

Identical with a short harness whip. Replaces the lungeing whip for close work.

THE REINS

12-14 m (39-46 ft) long and about 3 cm (1 in) wide, each prolonged at the fore-end by 1.5 m (5 ft) of 'halyard' ending in snap-hooks, or in buckles. The halyard runs freely through the rings; the reins are light and easy to handle. Their total length allows one to keep 6-7 m (6.6-7.7 yds) away from the horse and to describe circles of 15-20 m (16.4-21.9 yds) in diameter whenever the trainer moves.

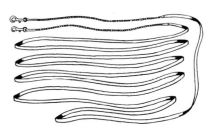

IV

INITIATION

Once the first rudiments have been taught by work on the lunge, and the horse is used to being girthed up, he may be fitted with the long reins, fixed to the side-reins of the cavesson.

THE VOICE

This is the chief aid at the disposal of the trainer at all stages of work on foot. The reins, the lungeing whip and the dressage whip are only accessories or correctives. So it is particularly necessary to take care of teaching by voice. Knowing that the horse is endowed with remarkably sharp hearing, interesting results can be achieved very quickly. Later, by associated reflexes, the classic aids (hands, legs, seat) progressively replace the voice, the least aggressive of the trainer's signals.

USE OF THE VOICE

Use clear language, steady and well differentiated on two planes: the words and their intonation. Conditioning of the horse depends on the trainer always using the same words for the same orders, and repeating them often. Steady, low tones used for long, 'drawling' syllables have a soothing effect; they help to restrain. On the other hand, short, dry syllables uttered in a sharper key act as a stimulus; they help impulsion.

Examples

1 'Walk' uttered sharply.
2 'Trot' spoken firmly.
3 'Gal-lop' or 'can-ter', in either case separating the two syllables.
4 In order to avoid confusion, tongue-clicking should only be used to keep a horse up to the gait at which he is already going.
5 'Tro-o-o-t', in a long, drawling and low tone, to bring a horse back from the canter.
6 'W-a-a-a-lk', uttered in the same way, to bring him back from the trot, and even more so, to reduce from the canter to the walk.

7 'Wo-o-o-ah', used in a firm tone to produce the halt, first from the walk and then from the trot or even the canter.

8 'Wo-o-o-ah', 'Wo-o-o-ah', repeated in very long syllables will be used to slow down the horse while maintaining the same gait.

The trainer will soon make his pupil understand him by being precise and strict.

IMPULSION

This, the prime virtue of all dressage, can be formulated thus:

$$\text{Impulsion} = \frac{\text{Response by the horse}}{\text{Demand by the man}}$$

And so, impulsion will ensue the more instantaneous and energetic the responses become, but also the nearer the aids approach to zero. Responsiveness of the horse, tact of the trainer.

To obtain these results and achieve perfect obedience to the voice, correct use of the *chambrière* (lungeing whip) is essential.

METHOD OF USING THE LUNGEING WHIP

The *chambrière*, or the dressage whip in work from the ground, are not to be considered routine aids, any more than the spurs are from the saddle; they supply the means of punishing idleness and summoning attention, but above all of sharpening obedience to voice and legs.

If the young horse is to respect the lungeing whip, he must first learn to have no fear of it. Do not proceed before he will tolerate contact (from nose to hocks), remaining quiet and still. This is especially important with nervous or ticklish horses.

Obedience to the voice will result from the following precautions in the use of the lungeing whip, which are less obvious than they seem.

1 Never use the whip before the voice. A reprimand inflicted on a pupil who does not know what is expected of him is a serious mistake on the part of the instructor.

2 Every time that the first demand does not meet with frank and instant compliance, follow up the voice with the moderate but instant use of the whip.

3 Voice and whip must cease as soon as satisfactory compliance is obtained; 'release on parole'.

4 Punish with the whip any slackening which has not been ordered. If the trainer continually nags with his voice at a lazy or negligent horse, he will bore him.

Adjustment in use of the whip – the trainer must take care to keep his whip still, without involuntary or disordered motions. When occasion arises he must pass it from hand to hand with slow and measured gestures.

According to circumstances and the temperament of the horse, the trainer will ration the use of the whip, limiting it to the minimum required.

1 Show the horse the whip: his attention is requested by pointing the whip at his hocks.

2 Raise the whip: the trainer lifts its point to the level of the hocks. (This is a pressing request for a response.)

3 Flick the lash towards the hocks. (This is a threat.)

4 Touch the thigh with the point of the lash. (This is a call to order.)

5 Bringing the lash round the croup from rear to front is a severe reprimand to the horse.

In any case, the trainer only uses the whip in order to do without it at the earliest opportunity.

ELEMENTARY DRIVING ON THE CURVE AND THE STRAIGHT

The first lessons are given to a horse which has been well relaxed beforehand, at liberty or on the lunge.

The outer rein goes across the back through one of the surcingle rings and is fixed to the outside ring of the cavesson. The inner rein slides in the inner ring of the cavesson and runs back to fasten on the surcingle. The rings halfway up the surcingle are used so that the reins resist every time that the neck is hollowed, and are taut horizontally or even yield downwards when the neck is arched.

This arrangement gives the inner ring a lateral effect comparable with that of the 'opening rein', thus permitting the bending of the neck firmly but gently. A feeling of direct opposition exerted by the cavesson on a horse lacking in lateral flexibility would be aggressive and useless. Instead of a bending of the neck, it would provoke either resistance or an over-bent posture.

On long reins as on the lunge the young horse tends to 'lie down' in the ring. He swings his head and neck outwards, turns about from lack of balance, lets the reins go slack, escapes from all control.

The trainer's first care must therefore be to impress on his pupil respect for the distance that separates horse from the trainer.

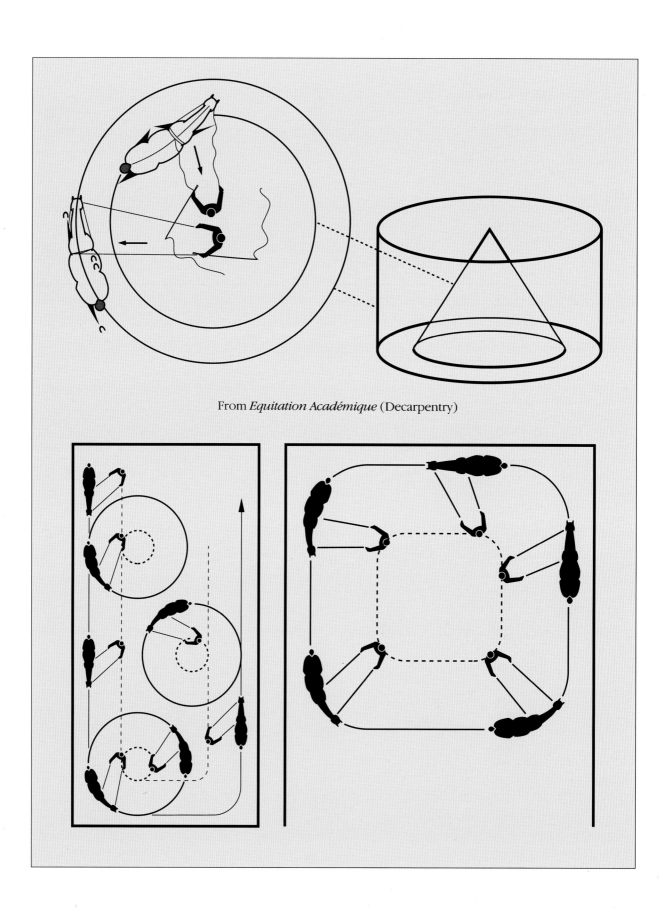

From *Equitation Académique* (Decarpentry)

To send the horse on to the end of his reins one must begin with the walk on the straight. To this end, the trainer takes up his position level with the quarters, to keep the horse in front of him and guarantee forward movement . . . he moves parallel to the track. The trainer will keep the horse away from him by making sharp undulations of the inside rein every time this is necessary. Thus right from the first lessons the horse will go straight down the track and right into the corners, always at the end of taut reins.

By means of the inside rein the trainer can bring the horse to describe a circle around him with his neck arched. At the slightest attempt to decrease the circle, the horse will be sent off to the right.

At this stage nothing could be worse than the horse turning vaguely around a stationary trainer. On the other hand, his attention is attracted by the trainer's movements, and little by little the pupil comes to copy the teacher's movements with his own. Working first on the right hand and then on the left, varying the sequence of walk, trot and canter, the horse from volt to volt ought to cover every square inch of the school, indoor or out. He describes squares with rounded corners. As the reins are lengthened he enlarges the circle or leaves it at a tangent. The trainer will combine transitions with these sequences judiciously, lengthening the stride on the straight and shortening it on the curves.

This working on the basis of repeated curves, regulated by the outside rein, brings the horse to an extension of the neck even before the trainer begins to act on his mouth – this is not a negligible factor.

As soon as the horse bends correctly around him on either hand at all three paces, the trainer can tackle

the preparation for changing hands. To do this the reins are arranged symmetrically.

The change of hand will upset the horse on two counts.

1 When changing hands the trainer will have to pass through the blind spot in the middle of the horse's field of vision, which often causes the horse anxiety.

2 The outside rein will pass behind the croup and wrap round the outside thigh, which takes many horses by surprise and sets off reactions which are often violent in the case of ticklish animals.

It is advisable therefore to prepare the horse for this by limiting the possibility of such accidents and their consequences.

1 With the aid of confidence, when the horse is walking straight, the trainer gradually moves across until

he is walking directly in the horse's tracks. Little by little the outside rein passes over the loins and the croup and finally slides along the outside hip. Now the trainer comes into the 'dead ground' of the horse's vision and speaks reassuringly to him.

2 If the horse runs away, start him on the wide circle and wait patiently until he has calmed down.

3 If the horse lashes out, keep the outside rein low and taut so that there will be no risk of its being caught under the tail. Thus, the shocks that result from this will act on the cavesson and **not** on the mouth. He will not be punishing himself seriously and order will be duly restored.

When the horse accepts the presence of the trainer behind him (out of kicking range) and tolerates contact of the reins along his body, he is ready to carry out the first changes of hand.

MANIPULATION OF REINS

The change of hand requires some quite indispensable precautions, on the part of the trainer, in handling the reins.

Holding the reins

Beginning at the trainer's end, they are looped uniformly at the right length. If too short, the loop will needlessly hinder the hand; if too long, there is a danger that the trainer may tread on them.

When both reins are held in one hand, they must be separated by the index finger.

To change hands from left to right

1 The trainer must be ready to take up about 1.5 m (5 ft) of the right rein and slack off a similar length on the left.

2 The reins being held together in the left hand, pass the lungeing whip behind your back into your left hand, which will be beside the horse's hip after the change of direction.

3 Stretch the right hand forwards as far as possible on the right rein before signalling the change of direction, so as to be able to give way on the left rein when it curves around the croup.

4 Once the change of hand is complete, the trainer is practically at the far end of the reins, the lungeing whip being on the side of the hips.

With practice, these motions become automatic.

ELEMENTARY CHANGE OF HAND

Suitably prepared, the horse is ready to carry out the first changes of hand at the walk. The long reins are still fixed to the side rings of the cavesson to limit the consequences if anything goes amiss.

The trainer begins at the walk by tracing half-volts and reverse volts.

HALF-VOLT

Having taken his horse down the long side, the trainer starts him on a curve around him. At the end of the semicircle he raises the forehand and quickens his own pace to get behind the horse who is travelling obliquely. The moment the horse gets on to the track again, the trainer moves back to the side. If the pupil is upset and tries to get away, he can be started on a circle by means of a corner of the school.

HALF-VOLT REVERSED

As soon as the horse leaves the track the trainer gets his head up and puts him on the oblique. He must quicken his own pace to cross the axis of the horse's advance and get on the far side of it. When the horse is some way off the track, the trainer puts him on to a semicircle which will bring him back to it. Tension on the outside rein will bring the head up and the horse will go straight.

To establish clear-cut figures at the regular gaits from the horse, the trainer must tread them himself beforehand, of course on a reduced scale, being careful to quicken his movements on the straight and to slow down on the curves.

In this lesson, agility and a sense of position relative to the horse are essential requirements for the trainer, since they govern the action of the hand to a great extent.

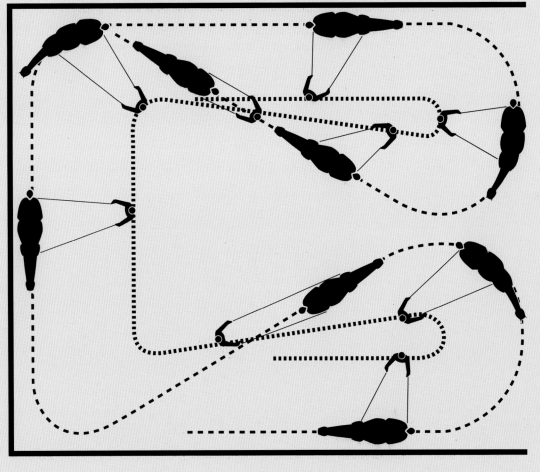

WORK IN A BRIDLE

Work in the cavesson has given the horse an overall handiness at all three gaits and a flexibility of the forehand that will justify considering the use of a snaffle.

At least in the initial stage I would recommend a thick-mouthed snaffle with cheeks (an egg-butt) because a thick bit is easy on the mouth and engenders confidence. The cheek-pieces stop the snaffle sliding through the mouth. They have the great advantage of reinforcing the lateral effect while sparing the mouth. For instance, take the situation of a horse working on the right hand with the right rein turned in. The order to bend to the right will be more effective and less hard on the mouth because the left cheek-piece, pressing on the cheek, will serve to push the head to the right. The trainer must endeavour to establish a light contact with the outside rein, keeping his arm very supple. In fact, the motion of the outer hind leg imparts a to-and-fro motion to the outside rein which will jerk at the mouth if the trainer's hand does not take up the shock.

Progress summary

On the circle. Bent by the inside rein, the horse describes a curve round the trainer whose presence level with the surcingle foretells the future role of the inside leg – shepherded by the outside rein which restrains the hindquarters and prefigures the use of the outside leg; his whole body is an arc.

Harmoniously bent in forward motion, the horse advances his poll which will be vertical to his mouth. Here we have the makings of a bringing to hand, the result of lateral flexibility in impulsion rather than forcing by the reins.

As the horse regulates his movements according to the voice and movements of the trainer, the hands' main task is to control the attitude of the forehand. Thus conceived and prepared, no-one can reproach the long reins for hardening a horse's mouth.

When lateral flexibility of the head and neck and bringing in hand have been achieved at all three gaits, the reins can be fixed to the snaffle at an equal height.

Thus it becomes possible to practise close turns on the curve, furthering flexibility and sensibility to the aids. Serpentines and work off the line will be the figures to practise at the walk and slow trot. The trainer walks straight ahead, leading the horse from this side to that of his axis of advance, gently bringing his pupil from one bend to another. These are just some of the lateral flexions which serve to relax, temper and strengthen the horse's confidence in the trainer when the latter takes up his position behind him.

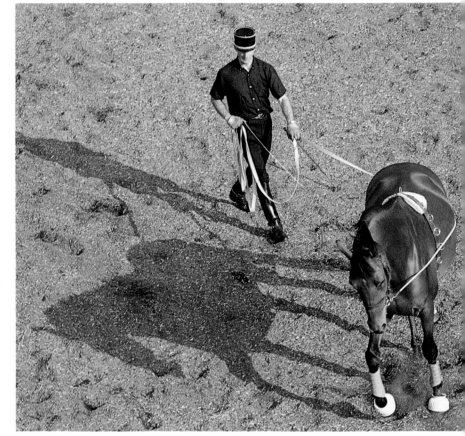

THE FIGURE OF EIGHT

Now is the time to consider the figure of eight; to perform it correctly calls for certain precautions.

Once the horse is properly bent and steady on the circle, new difficulties arise in passing rapidly from one circle to another.

When the horse enters the last quarter of the first circle, the trainer must quicken his own pace in order to cross over behind him and get to the tangential point by the time he embarks on the second circle. The trainer must be there just prior to the horse finishing the first one.

A horse will often avoid passing from one circle to the next by 'leaning' on the outside shoulder before turning his neck around. To avoid any undesirable haste, one must keep the horse's attention engaged by making frequent variations on the figure. For instance, disengage the two circles by insisting that the horse go straight on a tangent and wait until the trainer is behind him and has given the new aid to embark on the second curve. Recourse to such variations confirms the horse in his respect for the immutable rules: neck straight = walk straight; only turn with the correct flexion.

The figure of eight will be practised at the walk and the trot, often varying the diameter of the circles. It can be performed at the canter too, except for coming back to the trot or the walk for a few strides, just long enough to pass from one circle to the next and get set to start a new circle at the canter. The close alternation of starting to canter now left and now right will do much to improve calmness and balance in the horse.

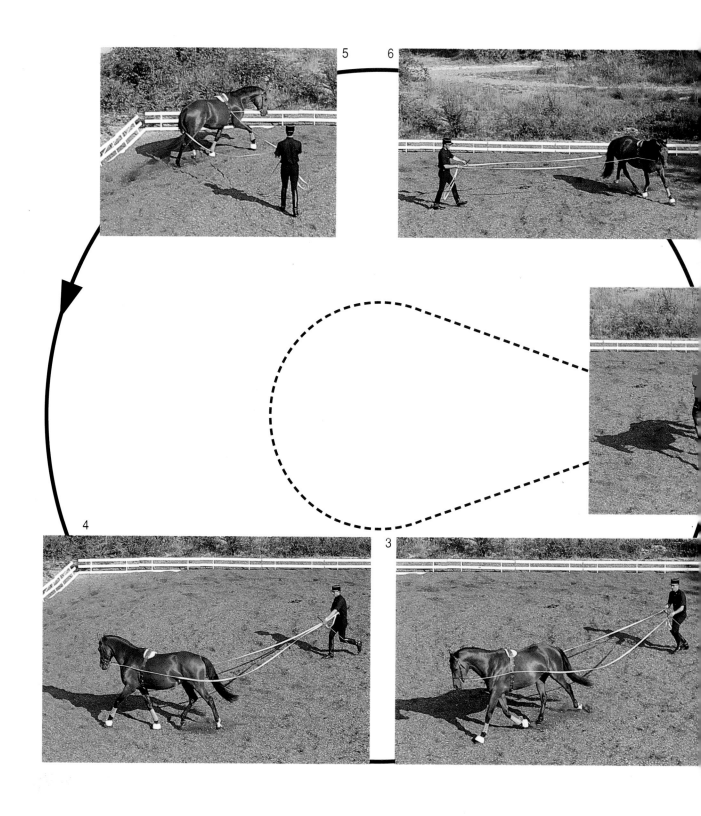

THE FIGURE OF EIGHT

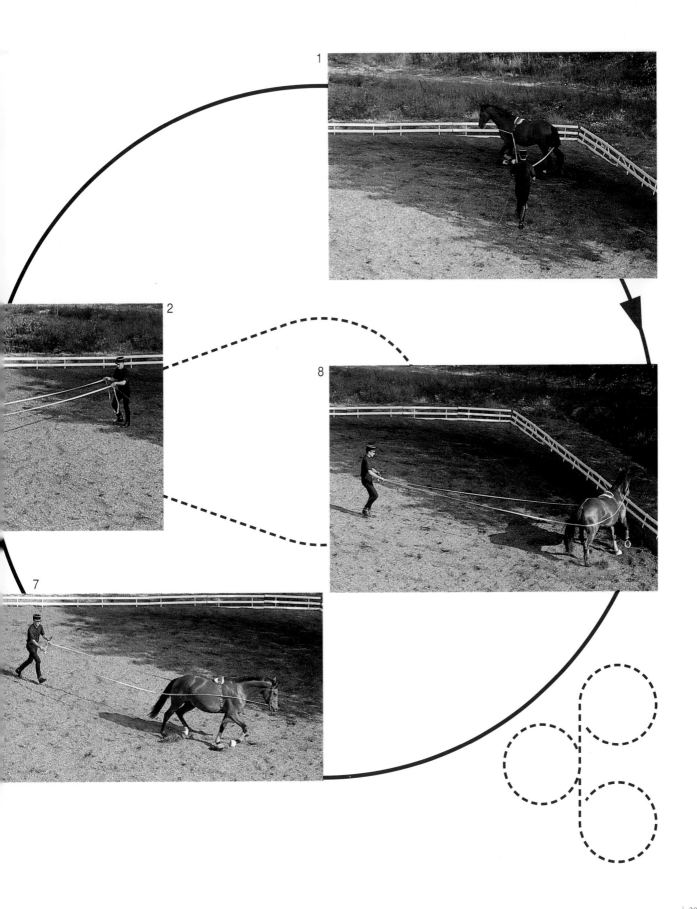

JUMPING SINGLE OBSTACLES

Just as the deception of the long reins enables one to submit a young horse to elementary schooling in the aids before the lesson in mounting, so it is possible to initiate him into jumping also. Just as at liberty or on the lunge, the horse bears no weight; so on the long reins the means of control will be much more accurate,

comparable with those that the instructor will use from the saddle.

For the first lessons it is recommended to return to the cavesson before passing to the reins of the snaffle. In either case it is advisable to reverse the inside rein, so as to keep the horse bound to the circle with the minimum of constraint whenever he tries to run out, as so often happens when one starts jumping.

The obstacle must be placed alongside the wall of the school, or the rail of the open-air ring, to set the approach in a frame. There must be no danger of the wings catching on the reins, which should slide over freely.

Having passed calmly over some ground rails, the horse can tackle small cavalletti which will encourage him to meet the obstacle at the mid-point from the beginning.

The horse's attention will be gained if he is put to a medium trot on a circle that passes quite close to the inner wings, then led to the obstacle by extending the circle.

The curved approach produces good balance on the part of the horse and gives him no occasion to take the obstacle in his line of sight and charge it. The quality of the jump is therefore improved.

The trainer must take care not to get in front of his horse on the approach. Then he must 'give' with the hands while the horse is in the air, urge him forwards to make his recovery and put him to a wide circle avoiding the obstacle. Bring him forwards to the walk and reward him.

When calmness and confidence are established it will be possible to tackle one jump after another on a wide circle, with or without returning to the trot in between.

The same exercise should be repeated on both reins. Since forword flexibility results from lateral flexibility, the horse which approaches the obstacle on a good curve will produce a more positive jump.

He will learn also to recover equally well on either leg, with more symmetry, straightness, and an equal distribution of effort.

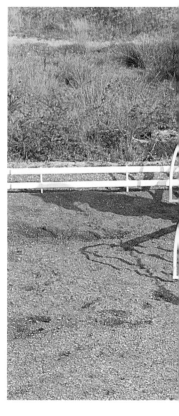

TAKING A SINGLE JUMP

DRIVING AND HANDINESS OVER TWO OBSTACLES

According to how soon the horse shows himself reliable and confident on both hands, the next stage will consist of linking two jumps by describing a figure of eight.

A bar and an oxer are placed opposite each other, along the two long sides, and the trainer can lead the horse from one to the other by changing the rein after each jump.

This exercise is practical for several reasons: it combines jumping an upright obstacle and a broad one, changing from right to left, making transitions from trot to canter and back.

A few simple devices compel the horse to take the jump in the middle, thus dispensing with the trainer's intervention which would worry the horse in his approach and spoil his jump.

This exercise develops handiness, freedom and style in a young horse, who must look on it as a game.

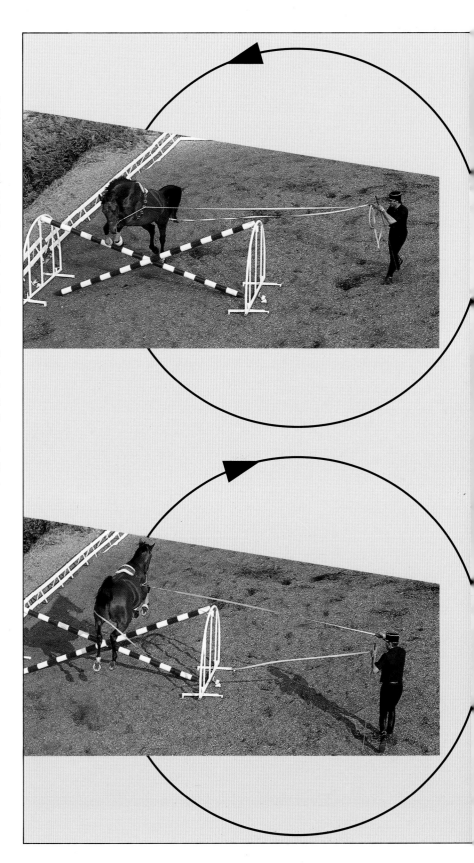

OUTDOOR SCHOOLING OF THE YOUNG HORSE

'People always want to go too fast in dressage. The way to get there in time is not to be in a hurry but to consolidate each step.' (Faverot de Kerdrech).

How many sensitive young horses of quality have proved dangerous to break? How many good horses have nevertheless presented serious problems, for the simple reason that they have not been properly and carefully prepared? The young horse who resists in the back will be so much the less up to weight: the one that is easy on the hand and flexible can be driven without difficulty; the one that accepts the long reins just around his haunches will not be at all alarmed by leg contact with his sides. Obedience to the voice leads to obedience to the aids, thus dispensing with crude disciplinary aids which only provoke undesirable reactions. All these conditions combine to favour exercise under the saddle at the earliest opportunity, in the open at brisk paces and over small jumps, taking all necessary precautions.

V

CONSOLIDATION

The long reins are a training technique to prepare the young horse for breaking to the saddle, but it would be idle to claim that they have the same merit for the consolidation phase.

On the other hand, work on the long reins can be continued side by side with training under the saddle. It allows an alternative technique which has the advantage of varying the situation, of practising what has been learned without the constraint of weight, of putting in perspective the elements of obedience that will justify an effective recourse to long reins when we come to the study of collection.

THE TRANSITIONS

Impulsion, lateral flexibility and handiness of the horse are now such that the trainer can consider improving his bringing in hand. If the reins were kept in the low position they would bring him behind the bit instead of encouraging him to raise the poll. They are now adjusted to a higher position, the outside rein passing over the back.

The concentration and rapid alternation of transitions from gait to gait which the hand and the voice produce together, will encourage progressive raising of the forehand.

Now that he has established confidence, the trainer can come closer to the horse. Thus placed, the trainer can see perfectly whether he is going straight and can work (on the straight) varied transitions from walk, to trot, to halt. The reins, together with the voice, and used by shaking or slapping the flanks and thighs, become aids to propulsion.

YIELDING WITH THE HINDQUARTERS ON THE CIRCLE

As we stated earlier in our section on the anatomy of locomotion, the bringing of one hind leg under the body is always connected with bending of the dorso-lumbar region. It is therefore only common sense to begin teaching this with the horse bent to one side on the circle. In this lesson the long reins play no part.

1 In hand, yielding of the hindquarters by direct flexion of the neck

The trainer stands beside the shoulder, leading the horse by the inner rein held close to the snaffle-ring. In this way he can command flexion, or reduce it by pushing the horse's head outwards.

With his other hand the trainer controls the hip by securing the outer rein which passes over the withers.

The trainer walks his horse around a circle of medium diameter

with measured strides, the horse being well bent around him. Every time the horse raises the inner hind foot he associates the pressure of the trainer's hand behind the girth with the whip touching his inner thigh.

The horse reacts by bringing his hips level, the hind leg coming obliquely under the body. In time, the pressure of the hand alone will suffice and the whip acts only as a call to order.

The exercise is at its most meaningful when the horse can go around the circle consistently making three

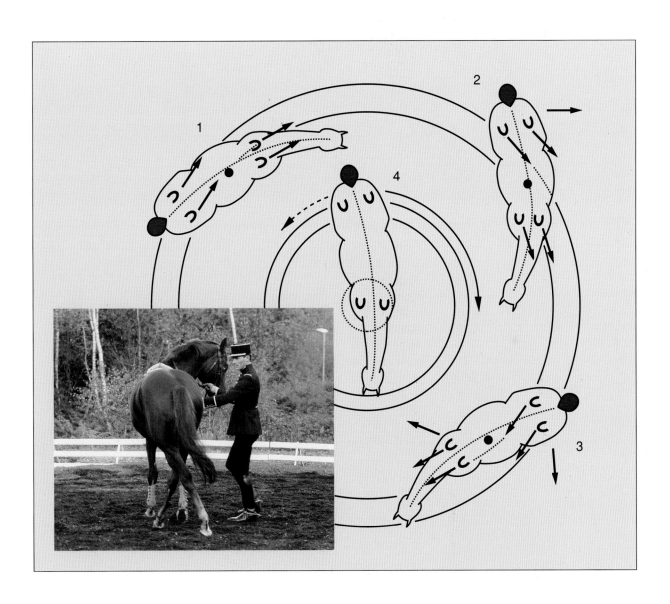

tracks, with the full engagement achieved when the inner hind leg is extended far towards the outer foreleg. Thus the inner hind leg applies the maximum impulse to the centre of gravity and ensures forward motion.

This exercise strengthens bending all round, supples and animates the whole hindquarter and prepares the horse to obey signals from one leg.

As the exercise causes a slight pivoting of the hips round the shoulders, it also causes a shifting of weight on to the forehand which makes the horse straighten and lower his neck. Therefore, it may be efficacious to bring to hand horses which resist extension of the neck, or even rear and balk.

2 Too much flexing: as we shall have cause to mention frequently in connection with work on two tracks, 'more is not necessarily better.'

In fact, if the trainer pushes the hips too far outwards the inner hind leg loses more ground forwards than it gains sideways, the croup tends to slide outwards (too much weight is taken on the shoulders because the inner hind leg is no longer working on the axis of the centre of gravity), and all-round bending suffers.

Consequently, this tendency must be avoided and is only justified very occasionally as an exceptional measure with horses that are particularly heavy and lazy behind.

3 Signal to yield by indirect flexion of the neck
Even if the trainer is to limit bending on three tracks, one-sidedness outwards increases the crossing of the inner hind leg, so that it becomes less fully engaged. The outer hind leg gains more ground but only by swinging outwards. For these reasons the croup tends to slacken

and forward movement will be difficult to maintain. If the horse is kept in indirect flexion he will turn by putting his weight on the inner shoulder, thus losing balance.

In summary, the systematic use of flexion is questionable. On the other hand, it may be useful as a corrective measure with horses that throw the head inwards in order to escape towards the outer shoulder.

4 Shrinking the circle.
The exercise culminates in the complete pivoting of the hindquarters around the inner foreleg. Its only purpose is to increase lateral mobility of the hips. There is maximum crossing of the hind legs but they are not engaged in any way. The horse turns entirely on his shoulders.

It is an exercise that may be used to stop a horse balking or rearing because it allows one to overload his shoulders, at the same time depriving him of what he relies on for disobedience – the use of his quarters.

5 The tight circling of the hips round the shoulders in indirect flexion is a nonsense. The horse knocks his hocks together or tries to 'dish' with his hind legs. It is a lesson in getting behind the bit.

Conclusion
In work under the saddle the rider may have recourse to this practice every time the horse refuses to bring his inside hind leg under him, resists the signal for flexion of the neck and tries to get out of hand. It is an exercise seen at its best when applied to the open side of the horse because it produces a bending round of the inner leg of the rider; this must act only on the girth and not behind it.

THE SHOULDER-IN REVERSED

After yielding with hindquarters on the circle, the next two-track exercise is the shoulder-in, to be practised on the straight. In principle, shoulder-in flexion involves moving the horse sideways in the opposite direction from the one-sided axis.

Basic precautions to be observed are as follows.

1 Prepare for the exercise by an overall harmonious one-sided motion. Avoid stiff backs and necks.
2 Limit the angle of movement to three tracks, so that the hind leg on the concave side pushes the weight of the body towards the opposite shoulder.
3 Here again, too sharp an angle will bring the horse on to his shoulders and tend to hollow his back.

With the long reins the trainer often profits by beginning with the study of the shoulder-in reversed.

The kicking-boards or the rails 'channel' the horse, blocking his attempts at escape forwards and saving him from frequent opposition to the hand. Thus the trainer can concentrate on the essential, which is one-sidedness and the angle of movement.

During the first lessons it is by the outside rein alone that the trainer can arch the neck and push the hindquarters on to an inner track. The inner rein and the whip are available to control any possible recalcitrance and set the horse going forwards again.

The second stage brings the trainer into position on the axis of the inner diagonal, close to the outer hip. In this position he obtains flexion with the outer rein and pushes the croup round by the pressure of the inner rein on the outer hip. This same rein, stretched over the horse's back, regulates the flexion of the neck.

When in the saddle, the rider bends the neck by the outside rein and regulates the bend by means of the inside one. He generates impulsion and urges the body sideways with his outer leg acting on the girth, and adjusts the placing of the hindquarters with his inner leg slightly drawn back.

Whether on the long reins or from the saddle, the shoulder-in reversed may be ordered at the end of a half-volt or of a broken line.

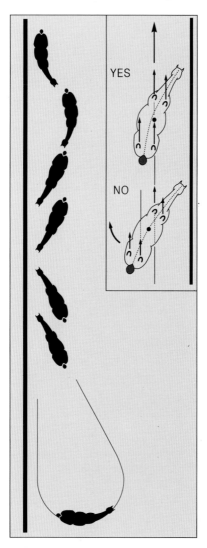

YES

NO

THE SHOULDER-IN

Let the father of the shoulder-in, Monsieur de La Guérinière, speak for himself: '. . . instead of keeping the horse dead straight from shoulders to hips along the wall of the school, you must turn his head and shoulders a little inwards towards the middle of the school, as if in fact about to turn; when he is in this slanting posture, ready to circle, you must make him walk forwards along the wall, helping him with the inside rein and leg . . . This lesson gives so many good results at one time that I look on it as the first and the last of all that one can teach a horse, so that he takes on utter suppleness and a perfect freedom in all parts of his body.'

The trainer now dispenses with the help of the wall or the rails. What are the advantages of this exercise?

1 The horse, bending around the trainer on foot or round the inner leg of the mounted trainer, is now going on three tracks.
2 At this angle, the inner hind leg comes obliquely under the body and alone provides propulsion, which serves to strengthen and supple it.
3 With the aid of such concavity, this hind leg comes underneath the centre of gravity, lowering the inner hip – a factor of recovering balance, the beginnings of collection.
4 The horse lightens his forehand and crosses the forefeet, thus freeing his shoulders.
5 Prepared by turning a corner, or by the volt in a good impulsion, the shoulder-in extends the gaits and gives the horse lightness. This exercise makes the walk more diagonal, will give quick and regular move-

ment to the trot and steady and collect the canter.

'The shoulder-in is the lesson above all else that contributes to collection, because the inner hind leg, moving along the line of the outer foreleg, steps towards the centre of gravity.' (W. Müseler)

Since collection and diagonalisation are synonymous, G. Steinbrecht is right to call the shoulder-in 'lateral flexion of the neck at the trot'.

How can one doubt that an exercise so easy to set going and yet contributing to bending, suppling and strengthening the haunches and lightening the shoulders, ought in fact to be considered as 'the first and the last lesson to give a horse', as La Guérinière said?

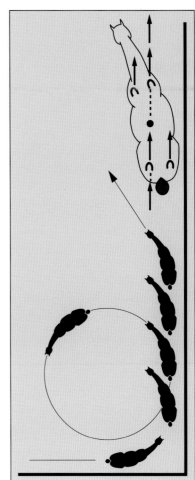

HEAD TO THE WALL

Having thoroughly taught the shoulder-in, the trainer can now tackle the half-pass. In principle this consists, for the horse, of passing obliquely in the direction to which he is bent. It is often beneficial to ask for the first half-passes in the 'head to the wall' position.

1 The horse's shoulders, set on the track and held in by the wall, are less elusive.

2 The hindquarters are pointed towards the centre of the school, so that the horse moves mostly on three tracks.

3 Working with the hind leg on the convex side, the horse is better able to thrust forwards than to bring his hocks under him, contrary to what happens with the shoulder-in. Thus it is doubly important not to aggravate this situation by an exaggerated angle that would disturb his balance still more by increasing the crossed-legs effect. In all these exercises on two tracks, one must be careful not to sacrifice the useful to the spectacular.

Prepared by a volt or the turning of a corner, the 'head to the wall' will be asked for as follows.

1 On the long reins, the trainer moves towards the centre of the school to contain the hindquarters by the action of the outside rein held low.

The inside rein maintains the flexion of the neck and will come back into contact with the hip if there is any reason to limit the obliquity of movement or to resume impulsion.

2 From the saddle, the inner rein gives the flexion, and the outer rein controls it.

The outside leg, working behind the girth, holds the hindquarters and pushes to one side. The inside leg, working at the level of the girth, is available to maintain direction and forward movement.

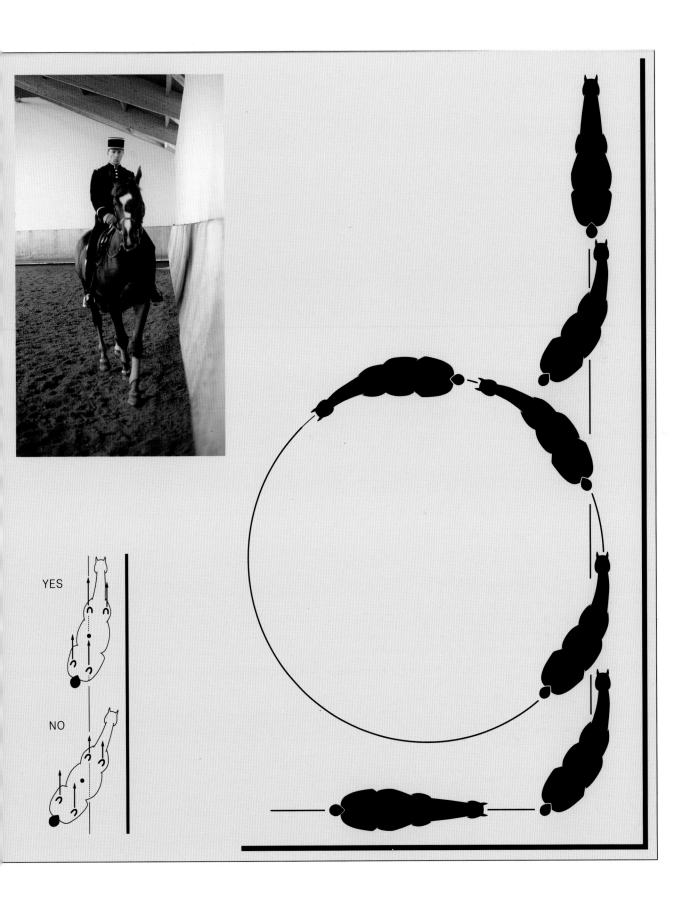

YES

NO

EQUIPMENT REQUIRED

As will have been seen earlier, keeping the poll raised implies a high position of the reins on the surcingle. This does not allow the trainer to contain the hips between them unless he walks close up to the croup, with all the physical risks which that entails in the first stages of training.

One solution to this problem consists in passing the lash of each rein through two pulleys which are fixed to the surcingle by means of snap-hooks. This arrangement allows the reins which come up low to the surcingle to leave it high. The pulleys eliminate friction and soften the contact between hand and mouth (an improvement on Mauléon's system). In this way the trainer can control, from a safe distance, the hindquarters of any horse, even a sulky or stubborn one.

THE HALF-PASS

Once the 'head to the wall' on both hands has been well and truly learned, both at the walk and the trot, the horse will be able to begin learning the half-pass.

The horse already engaged on a half-circle or in turning a corner will traverse obliquely in a half-volt or on the diagonal. To ensure natural paces in forward movement, the trainer must confine himself to such angles as will allow the horse to go on three tracks. The required crossing of the legs should be due to sweeping strides and not to excessive flexion.

By walking with long strides the trainer can keep up with a horse performing the half-pass at a working trot.

There are two schools of thought with regard to the half-pass in long reins.

1. **Trainer beside outer quarter**	2. **Trainer beside inner quarter**
Disadvantage: trainer is in dead angle of horse's vision: factor of anxiety for green horse.	Advantage: trainer is in horse's field of vision: factor of confidence for horse.
The hindquarters can drift away and the horse be at the wrong angle without the trainer being able to stop it.	The trainer controls all movement of the hindquarters and can correct and resume forward motion at any time by the inner rein.
To pass from the half-pass to the shoulder-in, the trainer must change the position and pass both reins over the horse's back.	To come back to the shoulder-in, all the trainer has to do is bring the outer rein back over the croup: quick and easy.
To carry out changes of hand on two tracks, the trainer has to pass both reins over the croup every time he reverses the half-pass.	For the same sequence of movements, the trainer need simply reverse the function of his reins without further manipulation.

When a procedure offers both a gain in efficiency and simplicity of execution, there can be no hesitation in giving it preference.

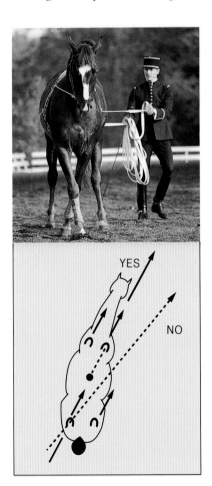

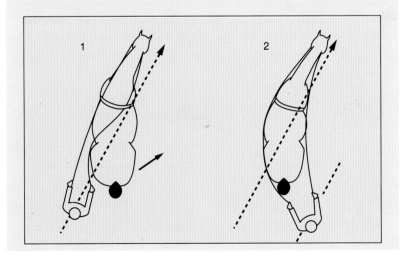

From the saddle, having laid the solid foundations of the canter and the half-passes at the trot, it is easy to achieve the first half-passes at the canter. At a constant angle of displacement, compared with the trot, the mechanism of the canter makes this exercise easier because it reduces the amount of crossing of the legs. It is thus that G. Steinbrecht has defined the half-pass as 'flexion at the canter'.

Of course, there can be no question of obtaining half-passes at the canter on the long reins at this stage of training, for the canter is not sufficiently collected to allow the trainer to follow his horse.

Coming back often to extension of the neck relaxes the horse and entails a supple stretching of the topline at all paces.

CIRCLING WITH HAUNCHES-IN

By 'haunches-in' we mean an adaptation of the half-pass, wherein the horse keeps his croup inside the circle described by the shoulders.

1 Since the shoulders must cover greater distances than the hindquarters, the motions of the forelegs become more sweeping as those of the hind legs diminish. This figure assumes a slight circling of the forehand around the hind legs, which induces the horse to shift his weight on to the hips – a step towards collection.

2 Once again it is to be observed that too oblique a posture favours the crossing of the hind legs rather than their engagement. This partly cancels the positive effect of the exercise and throws the horse off balance. The shoulders tend to get fixed and the hips tend to drift away towards the centre of the circle.

3 This turning of the shoulders around the hindquarters can be envisaged as an outward flexion of the neck; one then speaks of 'shoulder-in reversed in the circle'. (Cf. Ger. *Konterschulter herein*)

Because its use is limited to wide curves with only limited obliquity, this flexion presents a genuine corrective interest when applied to horses that refuse to keep their haunches to the circle and rake the neck inwards. In that particular case, the trainer can take advantage of an opposition between the shoulder and the hip on the outside.

4 When the horse's shoulders are turned in a direction contrary to the forward movement, the forelegs are obliged to cross markedly, and this together with the tightening of the circle may cause the knees to knock together. Thus, systematic and exaggerated practice of this exercise is unnatural and injurious. Even to the point of an about-turn on the hind legs, this movement compels the outer hind leg to pass behind the inner one and causes over-bending.

5 By progressive tightening of the circle with haunches-in, the horse increases lateral mobility of the shoulders by keeping the haunches more and more fixed. Eventually there will be a complete about-turn of the horse about the inner hind leg; in fact, a pirouette. This figure can be practised at the walk, then at the canter and then at the *Piaffer*, when the horse has attained a high degree of collection.

On the long reins

The trainer prepares the horse on the circle at an extended walk or a deliberate trot, taking up position right behind him. Moving up on the inner side, he secures the haunches with the outer rein and thus draws the croup towards the centre of the school. The inner rein maintains flexion of the neck, contains the haunches if necessary, and ensures forward movement.

From the saddle

The outside leg, drawn back, presses the horse on to the inside leg which, still level with the girth, maintains the overall curvature, controls the motions of the hindquarters, and propels forwards if necessary. The inside rein induces flexion of the neck, the outside rein checks it. Both hands either restrain or encourage the lateral motion of the shoulders as required, being carried either outwards or inwards. To balance the horse, the rider makes himself tall in the saddle, facing in the direction of movement.

JUMPING STYLE

'The horse's back is the bridge used to cross the obstacle. It must be allowed to arch itself freely in order to co-ordinate the take-off and the landing'. The words of one who ought to know, for the speaker is none other than Captain Caprilli, the father of modern show-jumping technique.

Having advanced beyond crossing small obstacles, now is the time to make the best of the effort expended by the horse by perfecting his style over more considerable jumps. At this stage, the trainer can further his pupil's progress provided that he is mechanically capable of being pushed on without a loss of confidence. As Jean d'Orgeix has shown in detail, it is the progressive shortening of strides on the approach that allows the rider to give the aid for take-off at exactly the right moment, thus giving the balance for

an arrow-like jump. The horse comes up to the foot of the obstacle, gathering himself together, which allows him to achieve the right trajectory and thus get the best possible results from his efforts.

Ground rails accurately placed permit the trainer to place the final footfalls at will, according to the shape of the obstacle (nearer for a broad jump than for an upright one) and the tendencies that have to be corrected (gradually increasing or decreasing the distance from the ground rail to the obstacle, depending on whether the horse tries to prop his feet or, alternatively, to attack excessively).

The horse which is brought up to the obstacle at an energetic trot on a wide circle, tackles it by adjusting his own balance, because of the curve and the ground rail.

The trainer should avoid any interference in the take-off zone and leave the horse at complete liberty.

Repetition jumps will enhance technique and confidence.

CONDUCT, TRANSITIONS AND JUMPING STYLE

By carefully arranging an upright and an oxer, the trainer can work out some interesting combinations.

In the figure of eight, the horse takes several different approaches; but they are graduated – landing now on one foot, now on another, changing the rein to pass from one fence to the next. The horse must shift his balance constantly as he returns to trot after every jump.

APPROACH, TAKE-OFF AND STYLE OVER THE JUMP

These exercises, once thoroughly mastered on the long reins, will be much easier to perform under the saddle.

When the horse has acquired a sufficient store of technique due to the use of guard-rails, the trainer can let him jump from the canter.

Whether it be on the long reins or from the saddle, the trainer will seek to modify the point of take-off when he considers this necessary, knowing that he can easily shorten or lengthen the distances, widening or narrowing the curve of the approach. With a course, jumps taken in the act of turning will ensure that the obstacles are cleared, and constitute an appreciable saving of time. This is vitally important when jumping on a circular course – it steadies the horse and adjusts the take-off, simply by adjusting the trajectory.

VI

BRINGING TO
PERFECTION

At the initiation stage the horse has strengthened his back by stretching it, thus suppling and toning up the top-line, in forward movement. In the course of consolidation he has developed lateral flexibility, tidied up any defects in going straight and improved his balance by practising exercises on two tracks and transitions.

Now all these gymnastic elements have been assembled for the bringing to perfection of the whole range of exercises that contribute to the rounding off of mobility and balance. These exercises, coming to the peak of their expression and giving style to the natural gaits of the horse, will give rise to the classical airs. The lesson of collection will be brought to its highest degree, and under the saddle the horse will once more show the ease and grace which were seen in him at liberty.

HALF-PASSES

As was explained above, the shoulder-in submits the horse to the aids on the inner side, bends him and settles his weight on the inner hip, whereas the half-pass submits him to the outer aids and develops lateral mobility. By rapid interchanges between these exercises, in the same bend, the trainer will be able to counteract any loss of flexion and imbalance on to the inside shoulder, which is so frequent in half-passes.

When collection is maintained (a shifting backwards of the centre of gravity and reducing of the base), the angles of displacement may increase. The half-passes will gain in cadence and expressiveness.

On the long reins the horse must keep pivoting round the trainer as if he were forever trying to pass in front of him, stepping out vigorously. Now more than ever, the horse must adjust his movements to those of the trainer.

THE REVERSE CHANGE OF HAND AT THE HALF-PASS

The half-pass reaches its perfection with the correct performance of the reverse change of hand.

The horse has to switch smoothly from one half-pass to the other, turning the 'slant' inside-out without loss of tempo. This requires a high degree of mobility, suppleness and sensibility to the aids.

On the long reins, as under the saddle, it is best to proceed in three stages.

1 Finish the first half-pass by straightening the horse's spine.
2 Set him on the new 'slant'.
3 Then set him going on the second half-pass.

EXAMPLE
On the long reins:

1 the trainer finishes the half-pass to the left by placing himself behind the horse and straightening him by tension on the right rein
2 still keeping behind him, he causes flexion to the right, thus bringing the shoulders in that direction
3 having established the right position, he moves up on the right side of the horse and starts him on the half-pass to the right by encircling the quarters with the left rein.

The means employed by the trainer, whether on foot or mounted, are completed to the extent that they conform to the same principle, though the circumstances may differ. The stance of the trainer plays a vital role, corresponding to the seat of the rider; pressure of the outer long rein against the croup pushes the horse to one side, as does the rider's outer leg when applied behind the girth;

the inner long rein, still in contact just behind the surcingle, controls lateral movement and ensures forward movement, just like the rider's inner leg against the girth.

Constant attention to a strict correlation between the aids induced by the long reins and those used from the saddle, causes, as it were, parallel movements with work on foot and mounted training.

The consistency of the language of aids is a better guarantee for assimilating new terms than the mere acquiring of conditioned reflexes, founded on what are merely conventions.

On the long reins, these changes of hand will be practised first at the walk and then at the trot.

Later, provided that the canter is sufficiently collected for the trainer to keep up with the horse by taking long strides, it will be possible to perform the same figure at that gait.

Knowing that a horse can only move sideways by leading with the leg nearest to the direction of advance (at the canter), reversing the half-pass will present a good opportunity to achieve the first changes of leg on the long reins.

THE PIROUETTE AT THE WALK

The pirouette at the walk is taught by progressive decreasing of the circle at the haunches-in until the shoulders pivot entirely about the inner hind leg, which ideally should remain on the ground in the same footprint. But since the haunches must remain active, it is advisable to confine oneself to a very small circle of the hind legs, which helps to maintain activity, thus preventing the inner hind foot from staying glued to the spot. This is exactly what happens on the long reins, because the horse pivots around the trainer, who is at the centre of the figure.

The smaller the circle, the more the forefeet cross and the less the hind feet cross. The nearer the horse approaches to the pirouette, the more he depends on the rider's inside leg or the inside long rein, which activates the horse's inner hind leg. The task of the rider's outer leg or the outer long rein is merely to restrain the haunches.

TAKING OFF AT THE CANTER: THE COLLECTED CANTER

As long as the horse is working in a circle round the trainer, the signal to take off at the canter is given by voice alone – first from the trot, then from the walk. The horse very soon begins to associate the foot on which he is to lead at the canter with the hand on which he is to turn and bend.

At the stage of perfection, the trainer may give the signal to canter to the right. He proceeds as follows for the right foot leading.

1 The horse is in front of him, attentive and walking straight and smartly.
2 He collects the horse by reining back and urging on to the walk alternately, changing frequently and decisively.
3 He puts the horse in position, slightly bending the poll by means of the right rein and lowering the left hand to bring the rein round the left thigh and imperceptibly shift the quarters to the right.
4 The command is uttered by voice and the horse leads with the right foot.

5 The reins return to an even level.

By the help of rehearsal, mere flexion to the right, with lowered contact of the left rein, will produce breaking into a canter with the right fore leading without any necessity to move the hindquarters to the right.

This taking-off at a collected canter from the walk, from the halt, or even from backing, having been already taught from the saddle, will be all the more easily understood and performed by the horse on the long reins.

INTRODUCTION TO THE PIROUETTE AT THE CANTER

By cumulative collection and progressive decreasing of the circle with haunches-in, the horse can come to perform at the canter the tightest change of direction possible – the pirouette.

This is an exercise 'in which a horse must be extremely free in the shoulders, and very firm and confident on his haunches'. (La Guérinière)

Logically, the ideal preparation for this would consist of making the horse capable of cantering on the spot ('marking time') and pirouetting at the *Piaffer*. Charles Raabe even considered that the *Pesade* should form part of this preparation. It is a most difficult air.

At every stride the horse has to bring his haunches under him without ever 'clinging' with the hind legs, and keep his forehand well clear of the ground while at the same time staying rounded and 'curved'.

As training progresses, the pirouette will be taught by stages – a quarter, a half, three-quarters of a pirouette, and so on. As Baucher used to teach 'Attitude before action', the horse must be collected and 'curved' before it moves. Thus it is that the volt of the old Masters (which was in fact a square described by the haunches-in) effectively prepares for the quarter-pirouette performed at every corner.

In the same way, a sideways flexion of the neck along the wall brings about the necessary conditions for a half-pirouette.

There is no technique of work from the ground that can claim to teach a horse the pirouette, but it is only the long reins that allow one to teach the rudiments in the capacity of a test or rehearsal.

TEACHING COLLECTION

$$\text{Collection} = \frac{\text{Impulsion}}{\text{Speed}}$$

This equation serves to show that in theory there are two ways of teaching collection.

1 To reduce speed at a high level of impulsion. In terms of driving a car, like braking with the engine.

It is a question of obtaining the *Passage* by slowing down the school trot, or the *Piaffer* by shortening the steps of the *Passage*.

Having achieved a high degree of impulsion in forward movement, the trainer progressively shortens the pace, taking care to maintain the activity by instantly lengthening it at the slightest sign of idleness.

By this alternation of effects, the trainer avoids the use of contradictory aids, thus applying the principle laid down by F. Baucher – 'Hands without legs . . .'

This is particularly suitable for teaching the *Passage* to horses that have a very lively trot with a long 'floating' phase.

In such a case, the teaching of the *Passage* may come before the teaching of the *Piaffer*.

2 At a reduced but steady speed, step up the impulsion. In mechanical terms, let the clutch slip.

If, starting from a very short-stepping walk, the trainer urges the horse on without letting him increase speed, the result is a slanting of the axis of advance, which gives rise to the beginnings of a *Piaffer* in forward motion.

Every time the horse tries to accelerate, the trainer calls a halt (or even a recoil), then resumes the shortening walk.

Here too, the aids are employed alternately, and the second part of Baucher's formula comes into play – '. . . legs without hands'.

By using this procedure one can also try for the *Passage* by giving impulsion at a very short-stepping trot. This gait is particularly useful for teaching the *Piaffer* to horses that have a daisy-cutting trot, not a spectacular one. In such a case, the demand for the *Piaffer* should precede that for the *Passage*.

Let us leave the last word to General Decarpentry: 'Whatever be the order in which the *Piaffer* and the *Passage* are taught, the greatest difficulty the trainer encounters in this work is always the transition from one to the other, *their linking up*, the perfection of which gives to the whole the greater part of its artistic value. That is why there is almost always an advantage in beginning to give style to the trot from both ends at once, that is to say by the *Passage* and the *Piaffer* . . .'

TEACHING
THE PIAFFER

With a horse in whose training a calculated proportion of work on foot has been included – progressively – the use of long reins may prove very effective in teaching the *Piaffer*. Because of the collaboration established beforehand between teacher and pupil, and due to the freedom of the shoulders in the absence of a rider, the horse will find it much easier to achieve the balance which this exercise demands.

The trainer builds up collection via free and ever more frequent alternations between the trot and the rein-back.

1 'Hand without voice'. The horse reins back, throws his weight on to the hindquarters, mindful always of breaking into a trot.

2 'Voice without hand'. The horse plunges freely into the trot, but is ready to halt at any moment.

3 When the trainer changes at will some diagonal steps backwards and forwards, he ceases to rein back by slipping in more and more impulsion by intermittent restraint with the hand. The horse advances less and less, but is more and more active. He diagonalises freely while making very slight forward movement.

4 The horse should complete the exercise with an immediate free trot, coming to a calm halt.

STAGE ONE

The trainer begins this lesson on the track in order to ensure straightness.

It is often useful in the opening phase for the trainer to stand on the inside with the outside rein passed over the back.

1 The horse has the trainer in his field of vision, so that an occasional

recourse to the lungeing whip will take him less by surprise.

2 The horse, beginning to rein back on the long reins, will more willingly step back as the trainer steps back, when he can see him.

3 The trainer is out of range of a possible kick, which would have to be punished instantly (scolding by voice and the lungeing whip below the hocks).

4 At first it is often convenient to tolerate and even encourage too low a flexion. This allows a horse to keep in hand and encourages him to maintain forward movement, but above all it helps him to bend his loins and bring his hocks under him without over-loading them. On the other hand, he will tend to stand under in front. This is a minor and only temporary inconvenience; it will cancel itself out later on when we progress to raising the forehand.

STAGE TWO
The trainer takes his stance behind the horse with the reins coiled.

1 He will still be out of harm's way.

2 With the help of the reins the trainer can channel and urge on the haunches much more accurately and efficiently.

In the course of work under the saddle, the rider causes the same changes to be made – trot, rein-back, *Piaffer* – bearing the following in mind.

1 Activity is determined by simple pressure of the seat and of the lower legs. At no time must the rider allow the horse to leave a leg inactive.

In case of idleness or inattention, the rider must correct this with a touch of the whip or of the spurs, followed by stopping the action of the legs.

The spur is no substitute for the leg, it simply prolongs it to make it more respected. Continual use of the spur bores the horse, instead of lightening the limbs, and often provokes undesirable reactions such as irregular paces and swishing of the tail, etc.

2 As the top-line is raised, supported by the hand, the rider is able to re-balance the horse and apply impulsion gradually.

As soon as the rider's hand yields, the horse ought to go on. At no time must the rider allow the horse to hang on the bit and force the hand, or abandon contact by going behind the bit.

What is called 'the French manner' (or rather used to be so called; it is now more often called 'classic') of holding the reins, gives great scope for the differing functions of the snaffle and the curb and lightens contact by varying the effects as required.

1 If the horse hangs on the bit, a mere raising of the hand brings the lifting action of the snaffle into play without any interference by the curb.
2 If the horse tries to get behind the bit, lowering of the wrist brings the effect of the curb into action, while at the same time relaxing that of the snaffle.
3 The principle of 'Hand without legs, legs without hand' applies. As the horse becomes increasingly responsive to the signals of the rider, action by the impulsion aids and the retentive aids can come closer and closer in succession without ever being simultaneous.

The vigorous bringing of the hocks under the body and the lowering of the croup, together with the raising of the forehand, lightens the shoulders and allows the trainer to slow down movement more and more without loss of impulsion.

As this proceeds, the horse is really marking time on the spot, and absolutely straight. All the power of the haunches is expended in upward propulsive force. All the joints bend with a spring. The action of the forelegs reaches its maximum height. The cadence is slow and majestic and measured.

The *Piaffer* '. . . puts the horse into a fine posture, giving him a noble and exalted carriage, making the motion of his shoulders free and bold and the spring of the hind legs soft and pliant: all these qualities are looked for in a parade horse and contribute to the good passage'. (La Guérinière)

PASSAGE

With the development of impulsion and flexibility, the horse is now totally responsive to the aids. The trainer can regulate briskness and speed of the gaits at will, can incite without speeding up or slowing down, without smothering the action. Thus the parade is a stylised trot arising from the best possible compromise between horizontal propulsion and vertical projection – 'The horse is held behind the hand as he makes himself taller, at the same time as his limbs glide forwards'. (General L'Hotte)

The longer the 'floating' periods

last, the finer is the cadence.

It is by alternately lengthening and shortening the trot that the trainer develops to the full the *Passage* in a horse that becomes more and more resilient. The air is better and the horse lighter when he 'quivers at the breath of the boot, and tastes his bit', showing himself 'diligent with his haunches and gallant with his mouth'.

By varying the contact, the rider can correct the frame and ensure lightness in hand. In time, the horse will be able to perform the *Passage* on the curb reins alone, at his full height, steady and relaxed, on the 'release of the aids'.

The horse must maintain regular cadence with symmetrical movements and utter straightness, whether he is performing volts, figures of eight or serpentines.

TEACHING THE PESADE

Total mastery of balance and the ultimate in collection are achieved in the *Pesade*.

Starting from the *Piaffer*, if the trainer increases the engagement of the hind legs and the lowering of the croup, there will come a moment when the legs are so lightened that the horse can take both forefeet off the ground and stay poised on his hind legs for a few moments.

Long reins can lend considerable help to a horse attempting this air above the ground.

1 The absence of a rider helps to establish the precarious balance required.

2 The trainer's position just behind discourages any attempt by the horse to step back, and thus keeps the hind legs engaged.

On the long reins, the signal is given as follows.

1 Repeatedly by voice and with the hands fixed to form a barrier, the trainer sets up a super-impulsion and maximum engagement of the hind legs.

2 When he judges that the horse is ready, he clasps the thighs firmly between the two reins, gradually increasing the tension on them. Thus encouraged to bring the body back without being able to release the hocks, the horse balances himself on the hind legs, raising the shoulders slightly with the forelegs tucked up.

3 The trainer maintains a firm contact with the hands to encourage the horse to stay in this position.

From the saddle, the signal is given as follows.

1 By intensifying the alternative actions of the legs, the rider brings the hind legs far under the body. In order to avoid all confusion with the school *Piaffer* and this preliminary *Piaffer*, he draws back the legs a little. This causes the legs to come close to the belly, nearer as the demand is intensified. This precaution ensures that the horse does not evade the movement later on, instead of performing the *Piaffer*.

2 When the horseman feels that the haunches are very low and the forehand very light, he presses with both legs. Then, keeping the hands firm and low, he squares his shoulders and asks with his back.

It is as if the rider were reining back by taking his weight into reverse, yet stopping it by the action of his legs.

To help the horse to stay firm on his haunches, the rider must necessarily take a firm hold. He must keep his thorax absolutely vertical in order not to disturb this delicate balance.

If the horse tries to over-bend, send him forwards immediately. If he is idle, go into a forceful *Piaffer*. If he hangs on the hand and comes down heavily from this figure, rein back, to the *Piaffer* again and start afresh.

For a good *Pesade*, it is important that the horse should go into and come out of the air slowly and gracefully, appearing relaxed and maintaining his roundness.

With practice, the haunches gain in strength and the horse in confidence, so that by the skilful use of his own balance, the rider can prolong the air and maintain it correctly with a very light hand.

'This lesson is used to teach a horse to raise his forehand lightly, to fold the forearm gracefully, and to stand firm on his haunches . . .' (La Guérinière)

WORK IN HAND AND ON THE LONG REINS

As we have just seen, work on long reins can play an appreciable part in teaching the *Rassembler* (the ultimate collection). It is the same with work in hand. Without entering into a detailed analysis here, a quick comparison of these two methods of dismounted work is useful.

WORK IN HAND

1 Taking his stand at the horse's shoulder, the trainer leads him along the wall or the rails.

2 The horse mimics the trainer's movements with his own, guided by voice and dressage whip. Control of frame and movement is ensured by curb reins held very short in a hand placed just behind the chin. As his whole body moves forwards on a firm hand, the horse raises his poll (vertical to the mouth) and gathers himself together.

3 The effect of changes between the walk, the trot and the rein-back is that the trainer can move, balance and collect to the point of inducing the *Piaffer* or even *Passage*.

It is possible also to do this on a snaffle, worked with one hand placed on the withers.

The *Pesade* can be taught in hand, with a horse that can perform the *Piaffer* well.

Curb reins are held evenly over the withers and the horse is completely flexed in hand.

Extreme engagement of the hind legs will be produced by the use of the dressage whip low on the legs.

When the trainer feels that the horse is ready, with his croup lowered and his shoulders light, he increases tension on the reins by turning his chest towards the haunches, and

blocks all movement backwards by the hocks by repeated touches of the dressage whip. The horse 'pours' his weight backwards on to his bent hind legs, which remain firmly on the ground . . . and we have the *Pesade*.

As in all work in hand, the trainer must take care to produce even results on either rein.

OUTLINE COMPARISON OF METHOD

Walking with contact

In hand, the trainer unquestionably enjoys more direct contact with the horse's mouth. He will thus have all the advantages of good hands – the ability to vary the frame at will, to half-halt, to vibrate the rein. Moreover, the trainer is better placed to observe the posture of the forehand than he is with the long reins. All this benefits from the work in hand.

Impulsion

By his very position, the trainer has the capacity to move the horse forwards, on the long reins, with the horse remarkably 'before him' in every sense of the words. In hand there is no such capacity except out of respect for the whip, which is less natural and more precarious.

Mobility

In hand, changes of position by the horse are strictly limited by those of the trainer, and he is not in a position that favours his mobility. This considerably reduces the possibilities of encouraging the horse forwards.

On the long reins, it is always possible to ease off the reins and send the horse forwards at a brisk pace on a wide circle. This is a major advantage.

Handiness

In hand, the trainer is, in practice, limited to a straight line along the track.

On the long reins, however, the whole geometry of school figures is accessible. The horse can *Passage* in a circle, in a figure of eight, and so on, and *Piaffer* in any part of the working area. This is a considerable gymnastic and psychological advantage.

Going straight

In hand, even if the trainer takes the precaution of working right- and left-handed, he is never in a position to make use of symmetrical aids. In particular, however 'scientifically' he

handles the whip, his use of it will almost always be one-sided. This often makes for lack of symmetry, resulting in irregular movements, lashing of the tail, hopping, etc.

On the long reins it is very much easier to keep the horse straight and regular in his movements because the hindquarters are channelled and impelled evenly and bilaterally.

In conclusion, these two techniques are obviously complementary, provided that the long reins are never underestimated or ignored.

TRADITION AND PROGRESS

It was in the reign of Henry IV of France that the equestrian vocation of Saumur was born, with the creation of a 'Protestant Academy'. There, according to Monsieur de Pluvinel, Monsieur de Saint-Vual was to teach the art of collecting horses by means of the pillars. Despite all the fits and starts of history, this vocation endures after four centuries.

Of course the School has had to accept the changing objectives and evolution of horsemanship, since this is an integral part of our cultural heritage. 'The cult of tradition should not exclude the love of progress', said Colonel Danloux, the chief instructor of the Cadre Noir who has gone down in history as having persuaded his country to adopt the modern principles of jumping.

When the practice of high school airs, derived from the most venerable tradition, is seen to be furthered by the employment of modern techniques less coercive than the pillars – such as long reins – can we perhaps perceive the meaning of this aphorism?

INDEX

anatomy 16-20

balance 15-16
Baucher, François 8, 15, 17, 79, 82
Borghese, Prince 8
bridle, work in 34

canter 14-15
    collected 78
Caprilli, Captain 62
Chamorin, Commandant 12
change of hand 32
    reverse 73-4
circling with haunches-in 60-1
collection 82
consolidation 9, 21, 47-70

Danloux, Colonel 94
D'Auvergne 13
Decarpentry, General 82
dressage whip 23
Duke of Newcastle 7
Dutilh, Commandant 18

figure of eight 37-9

half-pass 57-9, 72-4
half-volt 32
    reversed 32
head to the wall 54-5

hind legs, engaging 18

impulsion 26
initiation 9, 20-1, 25-46

jumping 40-5, 62-70

Kerbrech, Faverot de 15, 46

La Guérnière, F. Robichon de 7, 22,
    52, 79, 87, 90
L'Hotte, General 18, 20, 88
Licart, Commandant 11, 19
lungeing whip (*chambrière*) 23, 26-7
Mauléon 56
Maurice, General 15
Mazzuchelli, Federigo 7-8
Müseler, W. 52
Muybridge, Edward 12

neck, extension of 18-20
    raising of 17-18

Oliveira 11
d'Orgeix, Jean 62
outdoor schooling 46

Passage 22, 88
perfectionment 9, 21-2, 71-93
Pesade 22, 90-1

Piaffer 22, 83-7
Pignatelli, Gianbattista 7
pillars 7-8
pirouette 75-7, 79-81
Pluvinel, Antoine de 7, 94

Raabe, Charles 15, 79
reins 23
    manipulation of 31

Saint-Phalle, Captain de 15
Saint-Vual, de 94
shoulder-in 52-3
    reversed 51
snaffle 34
Steinbrecht, Gustav 11, 52, 59
surcingle 23

Terre-à-terre 22
transitions 48
trot 14

voice 25-6

walk 14
work in hand 92-3

yielding with hindquarters on
    circle 49-50